Kingdom Living BLUEPRINT

Gods Plan For You to Impact the Earth

Andre R. Jones

Copyright © 2013 by Andre R. Jones

Kingdom Living Blueprint
By Andre R. Jones

All rights reserved solely by the author. No part of this book may be reproduced in any form without the permission of the author. Any reproduction without the express consent of the author is unlawful according to the 1976 United States Copyright Act.

Unless otherwise indicated, Bible quotations are taken from the King James Version of the Holy Bible; the Amplified Bible, AMP.

Printed in the United States of America
ISBN 978-0-9911271-0-8

Published By:
ARJ Publishing Group
P.O Box 10649
Westbury, NY 11590

To reach the author:
www.AndreRJones.com

*This book is dedicated to my
Pastor, grandfather, mentor and friend, the late
Apostle John H. Boyd. Sr.
Words will never be adequate enough to express
the gratitude I have for God placing him in my life.
He saw the God in me, when it was just a seed.
His impartations have contributed to
the man of God I am today.
He taught me how to pray, fast and seek the face of God.
Thanks dad, see you when my work is done.*

Acknowledgments

I would first like to give a special thanks to my loving wife, Rachel. She has been with me every step of the way in making this book a reality. She has prayed me through as God continued to give me this revelation of the Kingdom.

I would also like to thank the New Greater Bethel Family. You were the first to allow me to preach this word out. This book was years in the making and I thank God for the many Friday and Sunday services, God gave us fresh manner.

Lastly, I'd like to thank Pastor Sunday. God used you to plant the Kingdom seed in me, you are a true Giant in the Kingdom.

Contents

Part 1: The Kingdom and the Church
    Chapter 1   My First Encounter with the Kingdom 3
    Chapter 2   The Counter-Culture 7
    Chapter 3   The Original Intent for Man 25

Part 2: Possessor of the Kingdom
    Chapter 4   God Chose Me On Purpose 35
    Chapter 5   Restoring Your Garden, Getting
                    Back Territory 43
    Chapter 6   The Nature of a Seeker of the Kingdom . . . 49

Part 3: The Seed of the Kingdom 57
    Chapter 7   Seed of the Kingdom. 59
    Chapter 8   Christ Brought the Kingdom 65
    Chapter 9   The Church in the Wilderness 73
    Chapter 10 Lessons from Kingdom Parables 81

Part 4: Spread the Garden
    Chapter 11 You Are the Solution 91
    Chapter 12 The Kingdom Is Not to Hold. 99
    Chapter 13 Kingdom House: a Kingdom Prototype . . 107
    Chapter 14 Kingdom Dominion. 117

Part 5: Finding Your Kingdom Purpose
    Chapter 15 The Kingdom Action Blueprint. 129

Key Kingdom Scriptural Reference 137

PART 1:
The Kingdom and the Church

Chapter 1

My First Encounter with the Kingdom

For the last year, I had noticed God changing my messages—my sermons had become more strategic and focused on the church's active role upon this earth. I was used to seeing the church through a more traditional lens. Throughout my experiences with church as I knew it, I had always been under the impression that the only responsibilities of the Christian was to just live holy, evangelize, and await Jesus' return. Church, as far as I knew, was about making sure your household was saved and being sure to attend weekly services.

One day, during my free time, I decided to flip through the Christian channels in hope of finding an encouraging word for a challenging season of my life. I had grown tired and frustrated with "church as usual" and knew that God was challenging me to rise to a whole new level with Him. I did not quite understand exactly what God was doing. This journey was rather daunting and uncomfortable. I felt as though I was trying to scratch an itch that could not be scratched.

After flipping past several channels, I came across the *God* channel and, within seconds, the presence of the Holy Spirit caught my attention and confirmed what He had been revealing and impressing upon me for the last year. This was the confirmation I had been waiting for! As I listened intently to the words coming out of the mouth of the guest Pastor, the expanded purpose of the church became more real and evident to me. I remember yelling, "That's it! That's what God has been trying to tell me for the past year!"

For the next six months, I made it my life's mission to read, watch, and study everything I could on this topic of the Kingdom. I researched and studied every Scripture with the keyword "Kingdom" in its text. The Holy Spirit took me to His University and schooled me on the Kingdom and its principles. The more I studied, the more the Holy Spirit began to reveal to me His plan and purpose for the believer. I was eating, sleeping, and breathing all things Kingdom. For the first time, I realized the grand plan God had for man. It was not to sit and wait for His return, but to occupy until the time of His coming as outlined in St. Luke 19:13. I had not only become exposed to the gospel of salvation, but now to the gospel of the Kingdom, which Christ commissioned us to preach.

Around this time, I was preparing to do a healing crusade in India. God had given my wife and I a passion for India and its people. What a perfect time for God to grace us with the revelation of the Kingdom. I believe this Kingdom message is a doubled edged sword. It not only possesses the power to prepare believers for eternity, but also, through its principles, to empower believers to transform communities, states, and ultimately nations!

The message of the Kingdom of God, which Christ commands us to preach, has gripped me and has become my obsession and life's mission. Everything I do—from preaching, to business, to missionary work—is done from a Kingdom perspective. It is through this perspective that God opened doors at the United Nations (U.N.).[1] This opportunity came through the revelation of the power and manifestation of the Kingdom of God in the earth. When I was first introduced to the message of the Kingdom, it started off as a mere seed that was planted in my spirit. Since then, God has allowed that seed to germinate and grow into a vast garden.

The message of the Kingdom is not just a message preached to the believer; it's a lifestyle. Throughout this book, you will be introduced to key terms such as "Kingdom of God" and "Kingdom Perspective" to name a few. These terms are associated with and will make up new ways of speaking and thinking as a citizen of the Kingdom. The Bible calls us citizens, those living in the Kingdom of God and living by Kingdom principles. The Kingdom is not a figment of your imagination. The Kingdom is not an imaginary phenomenon. It is REAL! Although you cannot locate the Kingdom of God in a natural geographical location, the Bible provides evidence that the Kingdom of God exists. According to St. Luke 17:21, the Kingdom of God exists inside every believer.

What I am telling you, in essence, is that the contents of this book is not just a book or another preached message; it is a culmination of my life's work and mission. These pages you are about to read are imbued with life and have the power to bring transformation and change to your life. I have seen, firsthand, the fully effective and transformative power of this word every single day of my life. It has become my life's goal to see the

---

1. The United Nations is an international organization of countries set up in 1945, in succession to the historical League of Nations, to promote international peace, security, and cooperation.

laws and principles of the Kingdom work in your life, bringing your life in harmony with purpose from a Kingdom perspective.

Through this text, you will be introduced to not only the Kingdom of God, but how you, as a believer, must position yourself to become fully engrafted and inducted into the Kingdom as a citizen. Each chapter of this text will provide nuggets of truth that will help you to walk in faith, to understand the heritage God has established for man since the foundation of the earth and the structure of the earthly kingdom we currently dwell in, to understand our assignment as citizens, and finally to learn how to infuse others with the message of the Kingdom.

Kingdom Living Nuggets

- Position yourself to become fully engrafted and inducted into the Kingdom as a citizen
- The message of the Kingdom is not just a message; it's a lifestyle.
- Opportunity comes through the revelation of the power and manifestation of the Kingdom of God in the earth
- The Bible provides evidence that the Kingdom of God exists.
- The Kingdom is not an imaginary phenomenon. It is REAL!

Chapter 2

The Counter-Culture

For many years, I was under the impression that the church was a sub-culture—a subordinate that is subject to and is a product of a greater culture. I thought, like so many other Christians in the body, that we were not to get involved in world affairs. Many of us use the Scripture—such as Daniel 4:17, Matthew 12:2, and Romans 13:1-10—to justify our lack of involvement within the society we live. We have focused on being "separated" and isolated from the world and its operation. When I came into the revelation of the Kingdom, I realized we were not a sub-culture, but a counter culture.

A "culture" is defined as:

1. The behaviors, beliefs, and characteristics of a particular social, ethnic, or age group.

2. The sum total of ways of living built up by a group of people and transmitted from one generation to another.

Our culture is the sum total of who we are. It is how we live our day to day lives on every level. Our cultural perspectives determine what we wear, how we talk, and even the people we hang around. In order for us to transmit the Kingdom into culture, it must be applicable to every aspect of our lives.

I heard a very influential and respected minister in our city tell the story of a very revealing conversation he once had with one of the mayors of New York City. One day, while sitting in his office, he received a call from the Mayor's office stating that they were discontinuing the liaison between the Mayor's office and the church. In response, he asked if the liaisons of the Muslim and Jewish faiths were being discontinued as well. The negative response and reason shocked him: Muslims and Jews were not considered religious faiths, but cultures.

I too was greatly astounded by this. Why hadn't Christianity been equated with one's way of living, one's culture? What is the difference between Christianity and any other religiously governed way of living? The answer is as eye opening and condemning as any I had ever faced. Unlike Judaism and Islam, the effects of the Christian culture are not distinctly apparent in our communities and everyday lives. The American Christian is nearly indistinguishable from the unbelieving American.

One of my favorite quotes as it relates to the Christian culture is:

> *"Because God's law has been abandoned by the modern church...it has first restricted 'Holiness' to things personal. Clearly, sanctification inescapably begins in the heart of man, but it cannot rest there. The man who is being progressively sanctified will inescapably sanctify his home, school, politics, economics, science and all things. By understanding and interpreting all things in terms of the word of God and bringing all things under the dominion of Christ the King."*
> *– Rousas Rash-doony, 1971*

Kingdom living must be transmitted into every aspect of our lives as believers. That's exactly what Christ came to do, not give us a religion, but a culture. With culture comes identity.

Luke 6:27-38 (KJV) – *But I say unto you which hear, Love your enemies, do good to them which hate you, Bless them that curse you, and pray for them which despitefully use you. And unto him that smiteth thee on the one cheek offer also the other; and him that taketh away thy cloak forbid not to take thy coat also. Give to every man that asketh of thee; and of him that taketh away thy goods ask them not again. And as ye would that men should do to you, do ye also to them likewise. For if ye love them which love you, what thank have ye? for sinners also love those that love them. And if ye do good to them which do good to you, what thank have ye? for sinners also do even the same. And if ye lend to them of whom ye hope to receive, what thank have ye? for sinners also lend to sinners, to receive as much again. But love ye your enemies, and do good, and lend, hoping for nothing again; and your reward shall be great, and ye shall be the children of the Highest: for he is kind unto the unthankful and to the evil. Be ye therefore merciful, as your Father also is merciful. Judge not, and ye shall not be judged: condemn not, and ye shall not be condemned: forgive, and ye shall be forgiven: Give, and it shall be given unto you; good measure, pressed down, and shaken together, and running over, shall men give into your bosom. For with the same measure that ye mete withal it shall be measured to you again.*

This was a cultural mandate based on Kingdom principles. These principles were—and still are—to be transmitted into culture by acting them out as part of our Kingdom culture—the counter culture.

Christ had the master plan to influence other cultures. When Christ chose His twelve, He did not choose twelve who were already in His sphere of influence. He chose twelve who had different platforms of influence throughout society. Christ knew He was an outsider to certain cultural circles and needed to be invited in, so He chose a tax collector, and fishermen just to name a few.

When Christ told Matthew to follow him, it was a strategic move to introduce the culture of Christ to that segment of the population.

Matthew 9:9-10 (KJV) – *And as Jesus passed forth from thence, he saw a man, named Matthew, sitting at the receipt of custom: and he saith unto him, Follow me. And he arose, and followed him. And it came to pass, as Jesus sat at meat in the house, behold, many publicans and sinners came and sat down with him and his disciples.*

When other people in the tax profession saw their colleague, Matthew, follow Christ, they decided to do the same. People follow familiarity. As a result, Jesus had access to people He would have never have had access to. It's the same with you today. Through you, Christ has access to people that your pastor would never have access to. It's the Kingdom formula.

Christ was great at ministering to the broken as well as the influencer. Take, for instance, the rich young ruler, Nicodemas, or the centurion. Christ knew how to minister to them in such a way that they would use their influential platform to project Christ. Heaven is not about a place, but more like a "plan." God wants us as believers to duplicate heaven on earth and the enemy wants his followers to duplicate hell on earth.

In the book, *Romanization in the Time of Augustus,* Ramsay MacMullen's claims what he believes is the formula for the spread of Roman civilization. It is one of the greatest examples of "culture" spread in history. He said:

"Roman civilization eventually appeared everywhere, as one single thing, so far as it was ever achieved. The degree of achievement, however imperfect, remains a thing of wonder, familiar to everyone....Never, however, was there greater progress made toward one single way of life, a thing to be fairly called "Roman civilization of the Empire" than in that life time of Augustus.......The natives would be taught, if it was not plain enough on its face, that could better rise into the ranks of the master race by reforming themselves – by talking, dressing, looking, and in every way resembling Romans. They would and did respond as ambition directed. They pulled Roman civilization to them—to their homes, their families, their world."[2]

The Kingdom culture is not sickness and oppression. As a matter of fact, wherever Christ saw anything that did not resemble where He was from, He replaced it. When He saw sickness, He healed. Where He saw lack, He multiplied. Deuteronomy gives us a clearer look at living the Kingdom culture.

---

2   Ramsay MacMullen, *Romanization in the Time of Augustus,* pp. ix-x, 134.

Deuteronomy 8:7-9 (AMP) – *For the Lord your God is bringing you into a good land, a land of brooks of water, of fountains and springs, flowing forth in valleys and hills; A land of wheat and barley, and vines and fig trees and pomegranates, a land of olive trees and honey; A land in which you shall eat food without shortage and lack nothing in it; a land whose stones are iron and out of whose hills you can dig copper.*

Deuteronomy 28:10-13 (AMP) – *And all people of the earth shall see that you are called by the name [and in the presence of] the Lord, and they shall be afraid of you. And the Lord shall make you have a surplus of prosperity, through the fruit of your body, of your livestock, and of your ground, in the land which the Lord swore to your fathers to give you. The Lord shall open to you His good treasury, the heavens, to give the rain of your land in its season and to bless all the work of your hands; and you shall lend to many nations, but you shall not borrow. And the Lord shall make you the head, and not the tail; and you shall be above only, and you shall not be beneath, if you heed the commandments of the Lord your God which I command you this day and are watchful to do them.*

That's the good news of the Kingdom! When you enter into the Kingdom (through Christ), there is not only provision in the afterlife but also here in the mortal life.

The Culture Seed

The origin of the word "culture" refers to preparing soil for planting and raising a crop. The word "culture" has its roots in the word "cultivate." A culture is simply the societal soil that is cultivated and worked through societal norms—or that which we allow to routinely take place. Each culture grows a crop (the results that we have in our society today).

Take, for example, some of the angry and sexually explicit music our youth listen to. Hip-Hop has become a type of culture, and with that in mind, it is only fair to wonder what type of crop this soil produces. The angry and dysfunctional families in our society are the direct result of the culture they live. The issues we presently deal with as a society are simply a result of a flawed culture, one without the values of God. Today's culture does not teach young people to obey their parents in the Lord. It does not allow parents to use the rod. It does not allow prayer and the teaching of Christ in our schools. The challenges we are dealing with have to do with our culture. In order to change the crop (results), we must change the culture (soil).

In the second chapter of Genesis, the Bible tells us that one of Adam's original assignments was to produce culture. When Adam sinned, he introduced another culture, one in which man would produce outside the wisdom and knowledge of God. Man, being made in the image and likeness of God, can produce, but sin created a culture outside of God's intent, one that originates in their own strength.

Genesis 4:16-17; 20-21 (KJV) – *And Cain went out from the presence of the LORD, and dwelt in the land of Nod, on the east of Eden. And Cain knew his wife; and she conceived, and bare Enoch: and he builded* *a city, and called the name of the city, after the name of his son, Enoch. And Adah bare Jabal: he was the father of such as dwell in tents, and of such as have cattle. And his brother's name was Jubal: he was the father of all such as handle the harp and organ.*

The Scriptures make it clear that Cain built a city outside the presence of God and absent of the wisdom, knowledge, and strength of God. They built a city in toil. We must begin to rebuild our school systems, families, and communities in the presence of God and not in toil and strife. God's presence is where the perfect solution lies.

It doesn't take millions of people to cause a tipping point. Jesus only needed twelve (really eleven) to turn the world upside down. God is still looking for dedicated believers to live this Christian walk of love and commitment to Him from the inside out. Culture is an continuously evolving product, resulting from people interacting with each other. It is created and than transmitted into society. This explains why Christ did not isolate Himself. He chose to fellowship with the extremely influential and with the poor man in hopes of transmitting what the Father had given Him.

The Seven Mountains of Culture

Culture is the soil, but there are those who stand at the top of cultural mountains who have become the societal and spiritual negotiators for these cultural mountains. Their decisions change laws, definitions, and distinctions, which we as believers are forced to live under. These demonic changing of laws makes life hard for the believer. That's not the will of God. A perfect example is found in the book of Daniel.

Daniel 6:7 (KJV) – *All the presidents of the kingdom, the governors, and the princes, the counselors, and the captains, have consulted together to establish a royal statute, and to make a firm decree, that whosoever shall ask a petition of any God or man for thirty days, save of thee, O king, he shall be cast into the den of lions.*

Those who were in power at that time wanted to stop Daniel from praying to his God, so they negotiated with the king to change the laws. The enemy looks to shift laws and times in the life of the believer. As a result of the laws being changed and Daniel staying true to prayer, he was thrown into the lion's den. Yes, we know God delivered him but he was thrown in the den because there was a demonic negotiator in the mountain of government.

God did not save your soul so you could just go to heaven. Every believer has been assigned to operate in some part of society. In the parable of the mina (talents), the owner rewards his servants, not with more talents, but with cities.

Luke 19:17-19 (AMP) – *And he said to him, Well done, excellent bond servant! Because you have been faithful and trustworthy in a very little [thing], you shall have authority over ten cities. The second one also came and said, Lord, your mina has made five more minas. And he said also to him, and you will take charge over five cities.*

The Bible says we are to disciple nations. When you, as a believer, show good stewardship over the gifts and talents God has given you, He rewards you with influence. The enemy has strategically placed people at the top of cultural mountains in order to be these influences.

Take, for example, Lady Gaga. She was voted in 2010 as the most influential person on earth. She has millions of followers on twitter and tens of millions watch her videos on YouTube. As a result of her influence on the cultural mountain of Arts/Entertainment, many Fortune 500 companies are eager to have her endorse their products to the millions of her fans and potential customers. Also, when our government overturned the "don't ask, don't tell" policy that prohibited gays in the military from revealing their sexual orientation, the first person United States Senators called was Lady Gaga. They called to thank her for using her influence in overturning the law.

Those who discover their sphere of influence have the ability to reach more people than the average preacher can, even if the preacher has a mega church. One of my favorite things to do is consult and teach churches on how to use their present resources to strategically place members in different spheres of society. I know of one church that sponsors youth to go to top colleges and universities throughout the country and then places them in the market place. Some of the most profitable companies in the country are open about being Christian based.

In February of 2011, CNNs website named the 10 most religious companies. At the top of that list was Forever 21. Now, I'm not going to get into a theological debate with whether you agree or disagree with the style of their clothing—I'm not a style guru, believe me—but one thing is for sure; they're not ashamed of the Gospel. Forever 21 serves millions of people a year, and on every bag they send out is the Scripture John 3:16. When asked about the Scripture, a spokesperson representing the company, responded that it was a demonstration of the owner's faith.

The popular fast food restaurant, Chick-fil-A, is also Christian based. Biblical principles have been the guiding light of their success. They also do something that all other restaurants would never do. They close on Sundays to honor God. As a result, God prospers them. I can name many more, but just these two alone have extreme influence. The Bible says, "One plants another waters, but God sends the increase"

So what are these seven mountains of cultural influence? These are the seven cultural mountains and their subcategories that shape the very fiber of every society.

Religion
- ☐ Church
- ☐ Missions
- ☐ 5-fold Ministries
- ☐ Bible School
- ☐ Discipleship

Family
- ☐ Marriage
- ☐ Parenting
- ☐ Motherhood/Fatherhood Roles
- ☐ Traditional Family Values

Government
- ☐ Local
- ☐ State
- ☐ National
- ☐ Military
- ☐ Law and Policy
- ☐ Lobbyists
- ☐ Ambassadors
- ☐ Social Services

Business
- ☐ Finance
- ☐ Manufacturing
- ☐ Retail
- ☐ Construction
- ☐ Sales
- ☐ Agriculture
- ☐ Health Care
- ☐ Transportation
- ☐ Food Industry
- ☐ Entrepreneurs

Media
- ☐ News Outlet
- ☐ Radio
- ☐ Journalism
- ☐ Marketing
- ☐ Public Speaking
- ☐ Technology

Art/Entertainment
- ☐ Theater/Fine Arts
- ☐ Dance
- ☐ Television
- ☐ Music
- ☐ Artisans
- ☐ Films
- ☐ Sports

Education
- ☐ Teachers/Professors
- ☐ Administration
- ☐ Curriculum
- ☐ Science
- ☐ Medicine
- ☐ Research
- ☐ Schools

These are the seven cultural influences that touch every sector of our present society. Every believer must discover where their influence is in one or more of the seven spheres affecting our society. Everyone is NOT going to be behind a pulpit in the church. I like how Dr. Cindy Trimm puts it: the church is to be the educational institution. Church is not a place where you come to have a good time until next Sunday, but the place where we come to get empowered to go out and effect change for the Kingdom of God. For so many years, we fought culture from the religious mountain instead of strategically placing people (believers) in all the mountains to bring about change in the culture.

The Church is the only institution that the Bible says that "the gates of hell shall not prevail against" (Matthew 16:18). It is an institution not built by man, but by God. He told Peter, "Upon this rock, *I* will build my church" (Matthew 16:18). Christ chose to build His own church, and to make sure it was managed right, He gave us His Holy Spirit. Christ loved and loves the Church so much. He calls it His body. It represents the manifold wisdom of God. Ephesians 3:10 (KJV) says, *"To the intent that now unto the principalities and powers in heavenly places might be known by the church the manifold wisdom of God."* That means we are the solution or the salt of the earth. Our methods and strategies preserve the environment, the integrity of doing business in the market place, and keep the family together.

This is exactly what Joseph was to Pharaoh. He was a solution. Genesis gives us an *amazing* example of true authority on a national level.

Genesis 41:38-41; 55-57 (KJV) - *And Pharaoh said unto his servants, Can we find such a one as this is, a man in whom the Spirit of God is? And Pharaoh said unto Joseph, Forasmuch as God hath shewed thee all this, there is none so discreet and wise as thou art: Thou shalt be over my house, and according unto thy word shall all my people be ruled: only in the throne will I be greater than thou. And Pharaoh said unto Joseph, See, I have set thee over all the land of Egypt. And when all the land of Egypt was famished, the people cried to Pharaoh for bread: and Pharaoh said unto all the Egyptians, Go unto Joseph; what he saith to you, do. And the famine was over all the face of the earth: and Joseph opened all the storehouses, and sold unto the Egyptians; and the famine waxed sore in the land of Egypt. And all countries came into Egypt to Joseph for to buy corn; because that the famine was so sore in all lands.*

Joseph became the spiritual negotiator for the cultural mountain of business and government. The world's systems—built outside the presence of God—need the wisdom of God to be injected into them. However, while the good news is that this wisdom is available, it's only available through the Kingdom. The Kingdom is not a place of greed and self-interest, but one of solutions that would restore the earth back to its original status of peace and unity with God.

Isaiah 2:2 (AMP) – *It shall come to pass in the latter days that the mountain of the Lord's house shall be [firmly] established as the highest of the mountains and shall be exalted above the hills, and all nations shall flow to it.*

This was the original plan for Israel. They were to be a nation of people that lived according to higher laws and principles, bringing about better results and productivity. The intent was to cause other nations to want to duplicate their culture. When Joseph or Daniel brought a solution to the king, they would acknowledge God. This moved the king and nation towards Jehovah God.

Proverbs 29:2 (KJV) – *When the righteous are in authority, the people rejoice: but when the wicked beareth rule, the people mourn.*

When you, as a believer, are in your place, the earth rejoices. We need teachers that are God centered to get supernatural results in the classroom. These results would cause school systems around the world to come to these believers for solutions just like they did for Joseph in the commodities market. Joseph was not only a regulator, but a creator of markets. Ask God to reveal to you your cultural mountain of influence.

"A Gospel that does not deal with the issues of the day is not the gospel at all." – Martin Luther

Be a Solution to the Culture

Your job is not your monetary source, but your assignment. You will hear me say often throughout the book that, work is your ministry. There are many of you who are well qualified to be somewhere else other than where you are, but God may have you there on assignment. God is your source, but your assignment (job) allows you to work out your Kingdom potential.

The first sign in determining where your mountain assignment may lay is an irritation of what's broken. People often ask, "I don't know my mountain. What am I supposed to be doing?"

I simply ask them, "What bothers you most? Is it a political issue? Social injustice? What bothers you with holy indignation?" When Moses saw his Hebrew brothers being treated wrong, it angered him. That discomfort became evidence of his assignment. There are things in our society that I knew was my assignment for the simple fact that I was bothered by how broken that area was. God caused it to grieve me so I would fix it.

I'll never forget the story my grandfather told about feeding the hungry. Our church use to give out food to those who were in need. One day, we were giving out food, and my grandfather (who was the pastor of the church) looks out the window and sees a young man get his food and then sit down on the curve to eat it, because he had nowhere to go. That bothered my grandfather. He felt, as human beings, we should be able to eat at a table with dignity. As a result, he went and looked for a building to turn into a food pantry with enough room for people to eat there if they had no place else to do so. Our ministry ran that pantry for over 20 years. This was the result of my grandfather, seeing a problem and choosing to be a solution to the culture.

Now, I'm not saying that people who are not in the Kingdom can't do nice things. But what I am saying is that people outside the Kingdom have limited access to the solution. Those "fix it" solutions can only come from God, but they will benefit all humanity. It's to show that a loving God wants the best for us all. Whose solution will you become? Who's waiting for you to answer the call? If not you, then whom?

Before I close this chapter, it is important that I say a word about education. Many people in the body of Christ see the importance of Bible College (which is extremely important), but not of receiving an education in the sphere that you will be influencing. I meet many people who say, "I'm not going to college. I'm going into ministry." Many times I look at them with sadness, because I know that, without proper education, they've just limited their audience. Part of the preparation for entering your cultural mountain is education. In the book of Daniel, when king Nebuchadnezzar besieged Jerusalem, he told his commanders to grab all those who were wise and understood science. Among those were Daniel and the three Hebrew boys. Their knowledge brought them before the king.

Daniel 1:19-20 (KJV) – *And the king communed with them; and among them all was found none like Daniel, Hananiah, Mishael, and Azariah: therefore stood they before the king. And in all matters of wisdom and understanding, that the king enquired of them, he found them ten times better than all the magicians and astrologers that were in all his realm.*

God was able to anoint and expand their existing knowledge. That's the key: *existing knowledge.* We must give God something to work with in order to become a solution to the culture. Knowledge in the finance world, mixed with divine wisdom and understanding from God will give you great audiences with great influencers. When I realized this point, having already gone to Bible College, I went back to school to gain more knowledge. My studies at New York University (NYU) have made me more useful and more knowledgeable to advance the Kingdom.

Kingdom Living Nuggets

- Culture is the sum total of which we are. It is how we live our lives every day, on every level.
- Kingdom living must be transmitted into every aspect of our lives as believers.
- Christ was great at ministering to the broken as well as the influencers.
- Culture is simply the soil, which gets cultivated and worked through societal norms.
- Christianity is not a sub-culture, but a counter-culture.
- Those who are at the top of their craft have the ability to reach more people than the average preacher can.
- Everyone's assignment is not in the pulpit.

CHAPTER 3

The Original Intent for Man

When Adam was in the garden, he lived a fruitful and Blessed, life. Once Adam disobeyed God, he would now have to produce under hard labor and work as a result of the curse. Genesis 3:7-9 says, *"And unto Adam He said, "Because thou hast hearkened unto the voice of thy wife, and hast eaten of the tree of which I commanded thee, saying, 'Thou shalt not eat of it,' cursed is the ground for thy sake; in sorrow shalt thou eat of it all the days of thy life. Thorns also and thistles shall it bring forth to thee, and thou shalt eat the herb of the field. In the sweat of thy face shalt thou eat bread till thou return unto the ground, for out of it wast thou taken; for dust thou art, and unto dust shalt thou return."*

Deuteronomy 28 gives us a look at the power of "The Blessing" that Adam lived under effortlessly in the Kingdom (Garden of Eden).

> **Deuteronomy 28:1-4, 8** – *And it shall come to pass, if thou shalt hearken diligently unto the voice of the LORD thy God to observe and to do all His commandments which I command thee this day, that the LORD thy God will set thee on high above all nations of the earth; And all these blessings shall come on thee and overtake*

thee, if thou shalt hearken unto the voice of the LORD thy God: Blessed shalt thou be in the city, and blessed shalt thou be in the field. Blessed shall be the fruit of thy body, and the fruit of thy ground, and the fruit of thy herds, the increase of thy cattle, and the flocks of thy sheep....The LORD shall command the blessing upon thee in thy storehouses and in all that thou settest thine hand unto; and He shall bless thee in the land which the LORD thy God giveth thee.

Christ came to empower and restore. The word "restore" *means:*
1. ***To return to its previous condition***
2. ***To put something back.***

Your Adamic nature was not born in a garden. As a matter of fact, David said, "In sin did my mother conceive me." This is why we had to be "born again." The new birth gave you life in a garden called the Kingdom of God! The good part is that the earth is eagerly waiting your arrival! According to Romans 8:19-21, *"For the earnest expectation of the creature –(creatures in the original Greek means creation) waits for the manifestation of the sons of God. For creation was made subject to vanity,"* or misery, vanity means misery, *"not willingly, but by reason of him who has subjected."*

Creation didn't willingly choose to be under a curse. The one who controlled it gave it over to the curse through his disobedience—Adam. Adam submitted the earth to the control of the enemy. Knowing this makes Christ's redemption even more meaningful and powerful. When Christ came, He not only came to save man, but the earth and everything that had been lost under the control of Adam. The Bible says in John 3:16, "For God so loved the world that he gave his only begotten Son." The word "world" in the Greek is *"cosmos,"* everything. It does not only mean people. Cosmos also means the trees, grass, animals, and everything within the earth.

So this Scripture actually reads, "God so loved the **earth and everything in it**, that he gave his only begotten Son." This is because everything in the earth was subject to the curse. Now that Christ lives in you, every time you speak, you release the earth from the curse. I'll prove it to you. Jesus didn't only speak to people; He also spoke to elements. His disciples thought He had lost his mind a couple of times, but He was actually doing His assignment. Sometimes people think you are crazy for believing what God said about what belongs to you, but you are not operating according to man's principles, but God's. Jesus spoke to the wind and the trees.

There was a time when Jesus and His disciples where on a boat and a storm arose. During the storm, Jesus was in the bottom of the boat asleep. When the winds became violent and water begin to fill the boat, the disciples ran to Jesus and said, "Carest thou not that we perish?" If you read it carefully, you'll notice Jesus does not initially respond to the disciples. Instead, he immediately spoke to the wind. The disciples did not understand that "life and death are in the power of the tongue" (Proverbs 18:21, KJV).

When the disciple spoke those words of death, they gave the storm power to take their lives through their confessions. Jesus had to take the power out of the wind before the disciple's words killed everyone on the boat, including Jesus. The enemy tried to use the mouth of the disciples to bring death before its time. Unfortunately, he's doing the same thing with millions of believers today. You must remember that the enemy is a "dead" spirit and does not have the ability to create. He needs your mouth to create. Why? Because he was not made in the image of God. Every time he sees your words come to pass, he's reminded of Whose image you're created in. Stop creating for the enemy and begin speaking the Word only!

Christ's words put the wind back in order since it was not designed to work against man and kill him. Everything God created was created for your benefit and enjoyment (1 Timothy 6:17). Why did Jesus bid Peter to come out onto the water during a different storm? I believe He wanted Peter to understand that the water was created to serve him and not the other way around.

Our church used to have a program that helped homeless people find shelter and jobs. There was a gentleman by the name of Charlie. Charlie had a really rough life. Charlie's been homeless on numerous occasions and has lived on streets and trains. He's been mugged at least three times since I've known him. When I first met Charlie, I would feel horrible for him and pray that God would turn things around for him. But after about a month of being around Charlie, I begin to see why Charlie had such a rough life.

No matter how beautiful of a day it was, when you asked him, "How's your day Charlie?" He would *always* answer, "Horrible!" I would try to encourage him, but no matter how much I shared God's Word with Charlie, he would always speak of how horrible his life was. I finally realized that Charlie was a victim of his own words. No matter how much I spoke positively, my words served me, but his negative words served him. Nothing would change until Charlie began to speak life into his own future.

Adam Locked Out of His God Ability

What was the true punishment of Adam when he disobeyed God? Lets look at Genesis 3:16: *"Unto the woman, I will greatly multiply thy sorrow and thy conception. In sorrow thou shalt bring forth children, and thy desire shall be to thy husband, and he shall rule over thee."*

This curse is a result of them not obeying the Word of God that had been given to them of not eating of the Tree of the Knowledge of Good and Evil. Here is their punishment. Verse 16 speaks of the results of the sin for the woman. Verse 17 says, *"And unto Adam he said, 'because thou has hearkened unto the voice of thy wife and has eaten of the tree of which I commanded thee saying, "Thou shalt not eat of it," cursed is the ground for thy sake. In sorrow thou shalt eat of it all the days of thy life.'"*

Now, I want to stop before I explain this and look at the word "sorrow." When we think of sorrow, it does not mean what we think it means. It says that the woman shall conceive in sorrow, but it also says, "In sorrow the man shall eat all the days of his life." So, if the pains the woman feels is her curse and God calls that *sorrow* that means every time a man eats a meal, he should feel labor pains too. Now, I bet the women are saying, "Amen." According to the Strong's dictionary, some of the meanings of "sorrow" are worrisomeness, toil, and labor. It does not mean that every time a woman brings forth that she will be in pain.

As it relates to man, it's always been thought that God cursed man. Well, that's wrong, because God did not curse Adam. The result of his disobedience was made clear in chapter 2 of Genesis, verse 17 (KJV): *"But the tree of knowledge of good and evil, thou shalt not eat of it, for in the day that thou eatest thereof, thou (man) shalt surely die."* That's the result of his sin. So what got cursed? The serpent got cursed and the ground (which man controlled) got cursed. Theologians assume Adam was cursed because he got kicked out of the garden and sin came into the world. But the Bible never says that man himself was cursed. The only person that became a curse for us is Christ. The Bible says, *"Christ hath redeemed us from the curse of the law, being made a curse for us: for it is written, Cursed is every one that hangeth on a tree"* (Galatians 3:13, KJV).

Man's sin resulted in his loss of authority and position in the earth—that ground, created to obey his voice, no longer recognized him. The God in him had been silenced. That's why the earth craves the manifestation of the Sons of God (Romans 8)! So now, his inability to operate in the image of God became his captivity.

This probably doesn't sound so terrible to many of us in this day and age because we are so far removed from The Blessing, but you must understand Adam. He was not created to need to work for his sustenance—that is not how God created you either. Your hard labor and toil is a result of you working a cursed ground that does not want to produce for you.

I think the Dakes study Bible sums it up well: *"This foretells the hard labor man was to endure making a living under the curse. The very elements were to be abnormal and make him suffer for his sin. Hard labor was to break him down physically, and finally result in his death. Deserts, barrenness, weeds, poisons, germs and every other form of curse causing adversity, were to add to man's punishment until he would finally return to the cursed ground himself. The planets were affected until weather conditions became a problem. Man's whole existence, until the final restoration of all things, was now to be one of constant hardship, sufferings and trials."*

This is why a manicured lawn, left to it self, will automatically begin to grow thorns and thistles. That is part of the curse of the ground (Genesis 3:18). In order to have a garden, it must be physically worked and planted. As beautiful as a garden is, it must be planted. God didn't want Adam to just live in the Garden of Eden, but to multiply it (Genesis 1:27-28). It's the same way in life. Its time for you to work your garden and get rid of the thistles and thorns that grows by default. Let the God part of you plant the garden you were designed to live in and then you can produce everywhere you go. Chaos, confusion, and sickness are not your environment! Peace, love and joy in the Holy Spirit are your Kingdom environment.

Man's confinement, to no longer operate in the image of God, which is what he was created to do, was his punishment. Whereas, prior to sin entering the world, he was able to speak to the elements and they had to obey him. Adam now has to work and till the ground just to get the same results he once got by just speaking to the ground.

Prior to the curse, whatever Adam needed, he would speak it and the earth would automatically produce it *without delay*. There was no delay. When God spoke, it happened—immediately. "Let there be light," and there was light. "Let there be this," and there was this. Operating in the image of God, in the God kind of faith, there is no delay.

One of the Jewish commentaries explains that if Eve had become pregnant in the garden, there would be no gestation period. She would have the seed and immediately give birth.

They believe that before sin came into the world, there was absolutely no delay in anything. The minute man spoke, it happened. I was amazed when I read that. Could you imagine walking in the fullness of God and your words having no delay in translation into action? I believe there's a place we can get to in the spirit where our prayers have *no delay*, not some of the time, but all the time!

Kingdom Living Nuggets

- The enemy is a "dead" spirit and does not have the ability to create. He needs your mouth to create.
- Man's sin resulted in his loss of authority and position in the earth.
- God had created a place for Adam where he could multiply his garden throughout the entire earth.
- It is time for you to work your garden and get rid of the thorns and thistles. Let the God part of you produce the garden you were designed to live in.
- Confusion and sickness is not your environment! Peace, love and joy in the Holy Spirit are your Kingdom environment.

PART 2: Possessor of the Kingdom

Chapter 4

God Chose Me On Purpose

When Jesus died and rose again, He destroyed every work of the enemy. The enemy, your adversary, is well aware of this. The devil, Satan, is a dead spirit. Remember, he does not have the power to create. The only way the enemy can create is to plant seeds, thoughts and ideas, in your mind and hope you will create for him. That is why you must set a watch over your mouth. Your mouth is your creative tool. You are a creative being! Stop speaking your problems, start speaking the Word of God (Your Kingdom Citizen manual).

God's Word is the language of the citizens of the Kingdom of God. When a person receives Christ into his life, he doesn't get saved solely to attend church. Once a person accepts salvation, he is designed to fulfill a particular purpose. This purpose is connected to the Kingdom of God. Each person is saved in order to bring about change in the world. Being chosen as an agent of change is not limited to book smarts or one's scholarly achievements. There is something in you that will cause God to "knight" you as a change agent in the world. God says to you today, "I can use you to bring about a great change in the world!" Each and every day that you open your eyes, know that you have been awakened on purpose and for a purpose. God didn't open your eyes and put breath in your body so you could be poor, sick, and live a troubled life.

He saved you so you could be the instrument of change. You may be the only one saved in your family—right now—but God saved you first because you are the one that can bring change. "Well, why didn't He save my sister? She's smarter than me." Your sister didn't have the stuff you've got. There's something in you! You were born and designed to be a warrior in the image of God.

> **Hebrews 2:5-8** (Amplified) – *For it was not to angels that God subjected the habitable world of the future, of which we are speaking. It has been solemnly and earnestly said in a certain place, What is man that You are mindful of him, or the son of man that You graciously and helpfully care for and visit and look after him? For some little time You have ranked him lower than and inferior to the angels; You have crowned him with glory and honor and set him over the works of Your hands, For You have put everything in subjection under his feet. Now in putting everything in subjection to man, He left nothing outside [of man's] control. But at present we do not yet see all things subjected to him [man].*

This is an extremely important Scripture. It says that when God put everything subject to man, He did not leave anything outside of man's control. Which means that if there are issues that seem like you have no control over, there is a something you are missing that has the power and authority to dethrone it out of your life. That word "subject" means to give control in a state of order. That means, when God puts things under your feet, He puts it underneath your feet in a state of order. He does not put it underneath you out of control. God gives you the ability to bring things under subjection. You cannot overpower something without first putting it in order.

You were built physically—everything in you was built— *to operate in the Kingdom of God and according to its laws and principles.* In order for you to live a life of true success, not driven by money or fame, but by the purpose God created you for, you must understand the laws and principles of the Kingdom.

And so, when I had began to study this deeper, there was a phrase that just kept staying with me that said, "The Kingdom of God is within you." We're going to take a look at that in a minute, but first let me make this statement: laws can be violated, but they can't be broken.

What do I mean by that? A great example of this is the law of gravity. In its simplest form, the law of gravity says that what goes up must come down. Although we may build airplanes to fly us around the world, the planes cannot stay in the air forever. It is still subject to the law of gravity. While it may temporarily violate the law by flying, it cannot break the law by staying in the air for ever. If any object is thrown into the stratosphere where that law is operative, it will sooner or later be brought under that dominate law. So, if you jump off a roof, eventually that law is going to win. So, it may be violated, but it cannot be broken.

According to Romans 5:12, the laws that God gave man were given to us for our benefit.

Sin was in the world before the law was ever given. Many people don't understand that the law was *not* put in place to hold you in bondage. The law was put into place to give you the liberty to act in the image of God. Some people see the law as bondage; God sees it as allowing His image in you to dominate the earth. It was to free you from the corruption of the flesh that you (man) could operate in the image of God unhindered.

However, man could not keep the law. When Christ came to the earth, he did what the law could not do. When you receive Christ into your life, all of the laws that needed to be fulfilled for you to operate in the image of God automatically became fulfilled. This fulfillment makes you a new creature and the righteousness of God.

Romans 5:17 – *For if by one man's offence death reigned by one; much more they which receive abundance of grace and of the gift of righteousness shall reign in life by one, Jesus Christ.*

You become a new creature; there's no more working to fulfill the law. Christ fulfilled the law for you. In the Old Testament, they had to fulfill all these things, and at the end of the fulfillment, they became a new creature. However, in the New Testament, Christ is your fulfillment!

Due to the work on the Cross, there is no more delay in your authority. He that is in Christ is a new creature. I cannot live contrary to how I was created to live in the Kingdom. You were built for Kingdom things. The Bible says, "The wages of sin is death" (Romans 6:23). That means you were not created to sin. So sin has no choice but to bring you death. Your body was not created to sin. Sin is a foreign substance, because you were created in the image and likeness of God.

When you study some of the spiritual causes behind cancer, you'll find out that there are some who have cancer because of anger, bitterness, or un-forgiveness. Bitterness and anger have the ability to produce sickness and kill you. You must remember that you were not created to be bitter, but to love. So, when Christ said, "The Kingdom of God is within you," He was not just speaking spiritually. Why? When He made that statement, He was not talking to Christians. He was speaking to the Pharisees, those who had not received Christ as their personal Savior. While they were trying to contradict His doctrine, they didn't even realize that the Kingdom was already in them.

Every person, no matter who you are, has been created with the DNA of God in him or her. You were built to live in the Kingdom. That's why there's certain things you cannot do without bringing death to yourself, because whether you like it or not, you were built for Kingdom living.

For example, everybody wants love. Humanity naturally craves love but when that love is forbidden or withheld, it creates problems. For example, there have been very successful studies done on the effects of neglected children. According to the US Department of Health and Human Services, the impact of neglect on a child may not be apparent at an early stage except in the most extreme cases. However, the effects of neglect are harmful and possibly long lasting for the victims. Its impact can become more severe as a child grows older and can encompass multiple areas, including:

- Health and physical development
- Intellectual and cognitive development
- Emotional and psychological development
- Social and behavioral development

What really is the origin of this desire for love and how does it relate to Kingdom living? Well, the Bible says, "God is love." So, to crave love is actually to crave God. You were built to crave God…who *is* love (1 John 4:8).

Jesus once revealed to a Samaritan woman that He knew all about her current living situation of having relationships with many men. He made it very clear to her that what she was searching for could not be found in human relationships. These men did not have the ability or capacity to give to her what she needed.

Think about it. If you were made from the earth but God breathed into you life as a man, then that means you have a God-like capacity in you. God gave man a capacity that would be impossible for "man" to fulfill alone. God is the only one with the depth to fulfill your longing. The Bible says, "Deep calls unto deep" (Psalms 42:7).

Christ continued his conversation with this woman by explaining to her that He could give her something that all the other men, could never give her. He was the water she'd been searching for. He was about to give her a drink of true love. You were built for the Kingdom, and who you really desire is God.

The enemy has deceived the world in thinking, that what you desire can be felt in a human-to-human relationship. In you is the DNA to live a Kingdom life. God did not make your body to function outside the laws of the Kingdom. Anything outside the laws of the Kingdom results in death.

God released to you the Holy Spirit, as the enforcer of the laws of the Kingdom, to make sure that you abide by the laws. Only by doing so, can you continue to function in the image He created you in—His own. The Bible is your "owner's manual," given to you by the Manufacturer. If I drive a Lincoln and I have an indicator light come on, I'm not going to look in the Honda manual for guidance. How foolish would that be? I would look in the Lincoln manual, because they built the car and know what and why the light came on. In addition, because they built it, they can best tell me how to fix it. As simple as this sounds, every day people run to someone other than God. If you need healing, who better to heal you than your Creator?

As you grow in God, there will be habits and appetites that will change. When you understand this, then holiness will result, not from what you do, but by being who you were created to be. Holiness is not about a "make me feel bad" message so you can live holy. Holiness is a reflection of Christ living through you in the earth.

Once you realize that the Holy Spirit lives in you, that you are made in the image of God, and that your body was not created to fornicate, then you will realize how unnatural it is to live contrary to the Kingdom. You were not built to be jealous. You were not built to hate. You were built to love. You were built for peace. That's how your designer designed you. You were built to solve problems not create them.

Kingdom Living Nuggets

- Set a watch over your mouth, because it's your creative tool.
- Stop speaking the problem and start speaking the Word.
- The Word through faith is the language of the Kingdom.
- You were built—everything in you—for Kingdom living.
- Laws can be violated, but they cannot be broken.
- To crave love is to crave God. You were built to crave God, who is love.
- God is the only one with the depth to fulfill the longing of man.
- Anything outside the laws of God results in death.

CHAPTER 5

Restoring Your Garden, Getting Back Territory

According to Romans, creation groans and travails for the manifestation of the sons of God. That means the earth needs you to speak in order to release it from the curse. God doesn't cause storms and tsunamis, the curse does. The enemy uses the elements of the earth to torment man, because man has not taken his rightful position.

I need you to see this; this is important. Man's curse, if you want to say it that way, was the fact that he could no longer operate in the image of God. So, when Christ came, He came to reinstate you to operate in the image of God and to be like Christ in the earth.

When one receives salvation, it is just the beginning of their Christian experience. Salvation is the door to the Kingdom. Christ called Himself the Way and the Door. However, we can't allow ourselves to stay at the Door. We must walk into the Kingdom by coming through Christ. Now that the washing away of your sins has saved you, you need to get into the manual (Bible) and learn how you were created to operate. The truth is you can be saved and still be in bondage. Many of us are like Lazarus was when he came out the grave—still wrapped in our grave shrouds.

Many years ago, Dr. John H Boyd wrote a book called *Coming Out of Your Grave Clothes*, and in that book, he explained that although Lazarus rose from the dead, he still came forth bound hand and foot. Old mindsets and wrong thinking will keep you in bondage. Jesus had to tell the disciples to loose Lazarus.

You can be saved and still be in poverty, sickness, and under the stronghold of oppression. The preparations for his burial and garments Lazarus had on hindered him from enjoying his resurrection. The Kingdom brings you into the liberty of being a child of God—the casting off of these old garments.

It's Your Assignment, Not Your Job

Some of you have skills that can be put to use more efficiently than your present job allows. You can easily be more effective doing something else. However, when you become Kingdom minded, you realize God didn't put you there to make money. Your job was never intended to just be your source of financial increase. Your work is your assignment. The money is a byproduct of doing your assignments. The Bible says very plainly in Matthew 6:33 (KJV), "Seek ye first the Kingdom of God and his righteousness and all these things shall be added to you." What are the "these things"? Daily provisions! The Bible explains that we should take no thought for tomorrow but let tomorrow take care of its self.

We've always heard financial advisors tell us to make our money work for us. Well, where did they get such a concept? They're not really that smart. It's a Kingdom revelation. This concept is embedded in us because we are in the image of God. We all know that money (excluding its economic value) in its rawest form is a natural resource, and paper comes from trees (stay with me, I'm making a point). Trees are a part of creation. So, if you work for money, instead of money working for you, you are working for creation. If you are made in the image of God, creation should be working for you. Anything other than that is out of order.

It is the enemy's job to get you trapped in the circle of a J.O.B (Just Over Broke). Now, I'm not saying you shouldn't work. The Bible clearly states that we're supposed to work. However, you were not created to work for money. You work to display the talents and gifts God has placed in you and to bring solutions to the earth. When you work, you show forth the image of God. This image gets "worked out" during your assignments. Working for money is not operating in the image of God since creation should now work for you. You should be able to speak and resources get released. You need to release creation from the curse—that's part of your assignment.

Speak and Declare

A major ingredient in regaining Kingdom territory is speaking and declaring. God, from the beginning, has been instructing man to possess territory (Lev 20:24, Num 13:30, Num 33:53, Deut 1:8). He told Abraham and David to possess territory. When you possess territory as a citizen of the Kingdom of God, you release it from the curse. He told Moses, "Get the people out of Egypt. I need them to go to a land that I have prepared for them. I need them to possess territory." But they were stubborn and would not speak what God told them to speak. They spoke what they saw, and not what He said to say. It's your job as believers and citizens of the Kingdom of God to speak the Kingdom language. Do not wait for your pastor or prayer leader. You speak it—out of your own mouth. In the Kingdom, you believe and then see, not see then believe.

Don't speak by yourself—teach your kids to pray too. I remember when my oldest son Uriah would get sick. He'd always say, "Daddy, I don't feel well." I'd tell him, "Even though you don't feel well, speak that you are healed in Jesus' name. You speak life." Being sick, he didn't always want to say it, so I bought him a prayer shawl and said, "Daddy's going to put the prayer shawl in the bag, and any time you don't feel well, you go get the bag. And when you get the bag, I'll know what it means."

Now, at first, I thought I was talking way over his head. One week later, he wasn't feeling well, and my wife knew something wasn't right. His body was fighting something as kids sometimes do. He told my wife, "Mommy, prayer shawl. Mommy, prayer shawl." He wouldn't say, "I don't feel well." He wouldn't say, "I'm sick." But he said "Mommy, prayer shawl."

So she got the prayer shawl and wrapped him in it, and he went to sleep wrapped in the prayer shawl. When he woke up, he said, "Mommy, I feel better. Mommy, I feel better." Now watch this: it's a principle. It is my job as a godly father to teach him how to speak in the image he was created in. You have to speak who you are. The earth belongs to you.

Kingdom Living Nuggets

- The earth needs you to speak in order to release it from the curse.
- Salvation is just the beginning of your Christian experience.
- The Kingdom brings you into the liberty of being a child of God.
- Your work is your assignment.
- When you work, you show forth the image of God in you that gets "worked out" during your assignments.
- Release creation from the curse…that's part of your assignment.
- When you possess territory as a citizen of the Kingdom of God, you release it from the curse.
- In the Kingdom, you believe and then see, not see then believe.

CHAPTER 6

The Nature of a Seeker of the Kingdom

This is the day and age that if you call yourself a believer, it is not enough to carry the Christian title. It is the presence of God in your life that will make the difference. Somehow, we have become disoriented and mesmerized by titles and have not understood that positions attracts warfare. So, if you are not ready for the warfare that comes with the title, just remain title-less servants of God (Matt 12:9).

It is my passion to empower the people of God to operate in the authority that God has given them—in every aspect of their lives. For me, it's not about a church or denomination; the Kingdom is my life. Kingdom living is not about having a title or a position, but about becoming an anointed father, mother, husband, wife, school teacher or entrepreneur.

In every aspect of our lives, we should be showing the authority that God has given us as Kingdom citizens and operating in that authority every second of the day. That's why it is important to understand the laws and principles of the Word of God. The Word of God helps us understand how God operates. An example is Romans 7:21. Paul said, "Then I find the law that when I would do good, evil is always present."

I constantly hear people say, "Every time I try to do something good, the devil is always there." Well, Paul tells us this is more than a coincidence. It is a law. So it shouldn't be a strange thing if, every time you go to do good, evil is present to deter you from the assignment that you're trying to accomplish. It's a law, but the great part of this law is: "Greater is he that is in you than he that is in the world." The greater One (Jesus Christ) lives on the inside of you.

Understanding laws and principles of the Word of God is crucial to winning in life. The Bible says, "Be not ignorant of the enemy's devices." You cannot be ignorant of the enemy's methods and the strategies that he uses against those who stand for righteousness. Nonetheless, let that Word of God be your foundation to what He has called you to do in the earth.

Becoming a Seeker of the Kingdom

Matthew 6:33 (AMP) – *But seek (aim at and strive after) first of all His kingdom and His righteousness (His way of doing and being right), and then all these things taken together will be given you besides.*

What does it mean to "seek " the Kingdom according to Matthew 6:33?

There are two very important parts to this Scripture. First, Jesus tells us to seek two things: His Kingdom and His righteousness. Secondly, the Scripture mentions the word "seek," which means to *hunt eagerly*. Let's look at a working definition for both of these commandments.

Seek the Kingdom: Eagerly hunting for the King's desire in influencing His personal will, purpose and intent, over His territory. It is producing a culture, values, morals, and life styles that reflect His desire and nature for His citizens.

Seek His Righteousness: Being in right standing with Kingdom authority and His way of doing things, which then puts me in correct fellowship with the King.

Being in right standing with someone gives you access to them and their resources. It's when you're not in right standing that those privileges are revoked.

I began to meditate on Scriptures like:

Genesis 1:26-28 (AMP) – *God said, Let Us [Father, Son, and Holy Spirit] make mankind in Our image, after Our likeness, and let them have complete authority over the fish of the sea, the birds of the air, the [tame] beasts, and over all of the earth, and over everything that creeps upon the earth. So God created man in His own image, in the image and likeness of God He created him; male and female He created them. And God blessed them and said to them, be fruitful, multiply, and fill the earth, and subdue it [using all its vast resources in the service of God and man]; and have dominion over the fish of the sea, the birds of the air, and over every living creature that moves upon the earth.*

Ephesians 2:19 (AMP) – *Therefore you are no longer outsiders (exiles, migrants, and aliens, excluded from the rights of citizens), but you now share* **citizenship** *with the saints (God's own people, consecrated and set apart for Himself); and you belong to God's [own] household.* This was the beginning of a journey in which I am still on today. This journey has caused me to write this book and preach the gospel of Jesus Christ not just salvation.

Colossians 1:13 (AMP) – *[The Father] has delivered and drawn us to Himself out of the control and the dominion of darkness and has transferred us into the kingdom of the Son of His love,*

Psalm 115:16 (KJV) – *The heaven, even the heavens, are the LORD's: but the earth hath he given to the children of men.*

It was the meditation on Scriptures like these, which will begin the process. Surrender to God and let the journey take you to the place that God has destined for you. When you look at all of heavens resources that are available to the Kingdom seeker, you began to realize that seeking God and His righteousness can only benefit you.

My New Nature

Romans 8: 19-22 (AMP) – *For the manifestation of the sons of God, For the creature was made subject to vanity, not willingly, but by reason of him who has subjected the same in hope, because the creature itself also shall be delivered from the bondage of corruption into the glorious liberty of the children of God. For we know that the whole creation groaneth and travaileth in pain together until now.*

Romans 5:17-19 (AMP) – *For if because of one man's trespass (lapse, offense) death reigned through that one, much more surely will those who receive [God's] overflowing grace (unmerited favor) and the free gift of righteousness [putting them into right standing with Himself] reign as kings in life through the one Man*

Jesus Christ (the Messiah, the Anointed One). Well then, as one man's trespass [one man's false step and falling away led] to condemnation for all men, so one Man's act of righteousness [leads] to acquittal and right standing with God..."

Did you see that? One Man's act of righteousness leads to an acquittal. That means you were in fact guilty and you should have been sentenced, but there was an acquittal.

The opposite is also true. It is effortless to sin, because you were born in sin. One man's mistake—one man's disobedience—and you were born into sin. As a result of man's sinful nature, after the fall, sin came as naturally as breathing. You didn't have to learn how to fornicate, gossip, curse, or lie. It all came naturally. It is your nature because of one man's disobedience. The Bible tells us that all have sinned and have come short of the glory (or image) of God (Romans 3:23). We all were born in sin and shaped in iniquity. As a result, sin became our nature.

If you believe in the power of sin and the old nature, then it is important to realize that such power came because of one man's disobedience. Sin became effortless. Likewise, because of one man's obedience, when you receive the redemptive work of Christ and receive righteousness by faith, doing right should also become effortless.

Paul proclaimed that when you come underneath the blood of Jesus, it is also just that easy to be blessed. You are working too hard. In your mind, you've built eight steps to being blessed or ten steps to being delivered. That's too much. All you have to do is receive the redemptive work of Jesus Christ and the Bible says that you are redeemed.

Genesis 1:28 tells us that God created man to give him dominion, power, and authority in and over the earth. He gave Adam the authority over all the earth. Once you become born-again, you have power over all the earth. There is nothing within the earth that you cannot dominate and you cannot rule. It is your Kingdom right! It is no longer a process of you ruling. You need to accept who you are. You rule and reign as a king in life.

If I'm a billionaire and I leave my son all my wealth when I go home to glory, he doesn't have to try and become a billionaire. He is a billionaire because I was a billionaire. It's the same thing once you become a believer in the family of God. Because Christ paid the price for you to be healed, you are healed. If you say, "With his stripes I am healed," then there's no *trying* to become healed. You are healed. We have made this too difficult. Many people are stuck in transition, thinking they need the preacher to lay hands on them to release them into their destiny. I'm not saying that its not a method, however, God says, "I give you power" (Luke 10:19)!

Let Your Words Do the Work

If you learn how to speak what God said about you, you will launch yourself into your own destiny. Jesus did not have to get the approval of anyone. The Bible says, Christ walked into the temple, opened the book of Isaiah, and found Himself in the book (Luke 4:16-21).

Stop believing what people say about you, and start believing what the Word of God says about you. People will try and judge your confession with your present condition, but they don't understand that what you are speaking is not who you are right now. You're speaking who He has called you to be. You call those things that are not as though they were (Rom 4:17). Confess, "I am blessed, I am healed, I am redeemed, I'm the head, I'm not the tail, I'm above and not beneath, I am rich and I'm not poor, I am who the Word says I am."

Sometimes you have to look in the mirror and speak to yourself. Call your own name and say, "I am blessed. I am favored of God. This is my year of the open door. Everybody wants to bless me." You must speak who and what the Word says about you.

You may be the only one speaking the Word of God. You'll feel like an oddball. You may seem crazy. Still, keep speaking what the Word of God says about you. Every time you speak it, you're giving it life. Every time you talk it, you're giving it life. Every time you announce it, you give it life.

Receive the finish work by seeing yourself in the "finished" work of Christ. The fact that you can see it means it's complete (Revelation 13:8, KJV). Let's read it, "Before the foundation of the world, the Lamb was already slain." This Scripture gives us a glimpse of how God operates. God always creates with the end already complete, and that's how He created you to create. Normally, when you have an idea, you envision the end result first and then work your way forward—before you even know how to put it together. You were designed to operate like your Father in heaven. If you can see it, you can speak it, and if you can speak it, you can create it. It's your God-nature.

God finishes before He ever starts. When God puts a vision or a dream in you, you never see the middle. You don't see the beginning. You only see the end. But if you can see the end, then that means it's already complete.

If you are in the image of God, you must understand how God operates in order to know how you operate. Or better—

how He has already created you to operate. So, if your Creator operates and creates with the end already in mind, that's how you operate too.

You'll have dreams and visions before you have money and resources. For example, when someone gets a business idea, they don't see the money first. They see the solution first and then begins to work toward that end. You may say, "Okay, I don't know how I'm going to do this, but I see it." You are in his image. If he showed it to you, it's already done.

Kingdom Living Nuggets

- Every area of your life should display your Kingdom authority.
- God gave Adam complete control and authority over the earth.
- You were created in the image of God and therefore must understand how God operates in order to understand how you operate.
- Stop believing what people say about you, and start believing what the Word says about you
- All of heavens resources are available to the Kingdom seeker
- If you learn how to speak what God said about you, you will launch yourself into your own destiny
- Receive the finish work by seeing yourself in the "finished" work of Christ
- The Word of God helps us understand how God operates.
- God finishes before He ever starts

PART 3: The Seed of the Kingdom

Chapter 7

Seed of the Kingdom

There's a powerful parable in Matthew 13:24-30 (KJV): *"Another parable put he forth unto them, saying, 'The Kingdom of heaven is likened unto a man which sowed good seed in his field: But while men slept, his enemy came and sowed tares among the wheat, and went his way. But when the blade was sprung up, and brought forth fruit, then appeared the tares also. So the servants of the householder came and said unto him, "Sir, didst thou sow good seed in they field? From whence have the tares?" He said unto them, "An enemy hath done this. The servants said unto him, "Wilt thou then that we go and gather them up?" But he said, "Nay, lest while ye gather up the tares, you root up also the wheat with them. Let both grow together until the harvest: and in the time of the harvest, I will say to the reapers, 'Gather ye together first the tares, and bind them and bundle them and burn them: but gather the wheat unto my barn.'"*

I've always heard people apply this Scripture to the church. However, Matthew begins by saying, "The Kingdom of heaven is likened unto..."He didn't say the "church." He said the "Kingdom."

After Jesus finished telling the parable, He sent the multitude away. The disciples were totally confused and didn't know what was going on. "At which time the disciples asked Christ to explain the parable."

Christ responds to their request by saying, "He that soweth the good seed is the Son of man; the field is the world, he that soweth the seed is the Son of man; the good seed are the children of the Kingdom; but the tares are the children of the wicked one. The enemy that sowed them is the devil; the harvest is the end of the world; and the reapers are the angels."

The Bible makes it clear that the earth has been given to the people of God. The children of the Kingdom own the field—the world. The children of the Kingdom of God own the Kingdoms of the world. *You* own the world. However, the Scripture is very clear that the enemy has planted tares in the earth because the citizens didn't know who they were or what they had.

Now that people are awakening to the Kingdom of God, there are some who feel we should get rid of everybody in the world that's not saved. However, through this parable, Christ makes it clear that doing so is not possible. The tares have been embedded into our society and to remove them would collapse this current system.

You can't get rid of every unsaved corporation. You can't get rid of every unsaved politician. The wheat and the tares must grow together.

I've heard people say, "I would never do business with an unbeliever." Well, your landlord probably isn't saved. You're doing business with him every time you pay your rent. Con Edison (a power company in NY) isn't owned by Christians, but you pay that bill every month, because if you don't, you'll be sitting in the dark. The same goes for banks and department stores.

However, in the end, when the trumpet blows, He'll call for the tares first and remove them from the scene (Matt 13:31). Until then, know what your position in the earth as a believer and creator is. Know who you are. Know how you've been designed to function and create in the earth. Bring heaven to earth through your Kingdom ability.

You don't need to follow eight steps to get a miracle. You need to learn how to create and operate in the earth as a Kingdom citizen. You need to read the manual (the Bible) and know who you are in the Word of God.

In the book of Exodus, God told Moses to possess Canaan. Why would God give him a command to possess a land that had giants in it? I believe His answer is our answer. There are industries you must possess that have giants in it, but God has given you power to subdue those giants.

Whatever territory God has called you to claim, whatever your business, there will be giants you must overcome. Remember, the end was finished before the beginning. However, be confidant that God has already given you the power to complete the assignment. All you have to do is *become*. Become who He said you are. Understand the laws and the principles…become the Word. Become the head and not the tail. Become above and not beneath, rich and not poor. Become the Word.

Jesus took thousands of years to speak through prophets of His coming. Right before the seed of the King was about to be planted, Gabriel came to Mary and gave her a Word. Her response to that Word was, "Be it unto me according to thy word."

I believe with all my heart that Mary conceived at the point she received the Word. When a woman first gets pregnant, she may not know for months that she is pregnant. Mary had no quick evidence. She had to receive it even when she couldn't feel it. She told Elizabeth. She told Joseph. She told everybody and the Word became flesh. You must speak the Word, until the Word of God spoken out of your mouth, produces everything around you.

Everything you see manifested in the earth today came from within the earth—buildings, cars, clothing, money, and so on. All of this was in the earth and came out of the dust and its elements. So, you're not speaking to cars. You're speaking to creation.

This earth was just green land—trees, deserts, and streams to the natural eye. But when man begins to see and to speak, things came out of it. Science and chemistry began to go to work in order to produce what man saw and spoke. These are principles God gave man in order that man might have dominion. Those who have not yet accepted Christ as their personal Savior are using these principles to produce. But I believe the lion in you (the Believer) is about to roar.

Kingdom Nuggets

- The tares (representing the unbelievers) have been embedded into our society and to remove them would collapse this current system.
- You've been designed to function and create in the earth.
- Learn how to create and operate in the earth as a Kingdom citizen.
- God has given you power to subdue giants.
- All you have to do is become.
- Everything you see manifested in the earth today came from within the earth
- Bring heaven to earth through your Kingdom ability.
- Whatever territory God has called you to claim, there will be giants you must overcome
- Be confidant that God has already given you the power to complete the assignment.

CHAPTER 8

Christ Brought the Kingdom

When Christ came to the earth, He did not leave the Kingdom behind in heaven. When Christ came to earth from heaven, He brought the Kingdom with Him. When He would do miracles, Christ would say, "The Kingdom has come unto you."

How do you know the Kingdom is here? Every time someone gets healed, delivered, or set free in the name of Jesus, that's proof that the Kingdom has arrived and been restored. To deny the power and presence of miracles in this day and age is to deny that the Kingdom is here.

Every time blind eyes would open, Jesus was saying that the Kingdom had come. When the withered hand grew back, the Kingdom had come. When Lazarus was raised from the dead, the Kingdom had come. When He multiplied fish and bread, the Kingdom had come. You travel with the full backing of the Kingdom—just as Christ did.

> **Matthew 12:28-29,** (AMP) – *"But if it is by the Spirit of God that I drive out the demons, then the Kingdom of God has come upon you before you expected it. Or how can a person go into a strong man's house and carry off his goods, the entire equipment of his house,*

without first binding the strong man? Then indeed, he may plunder his house."

The fact that miracles are still happening says two things. One, the Kingdom is here. Two, the Kingdom could not release its resources unless that spirit or strongman that once held the earth in captivity was already bound up.

In order for anything of the Kingdom to get to you, you must first bind up the strong man over the situation in order to receive the release.

Mark 3:26-28 (KJV) – *And if Satan rise up against himself, and be divided, he cannot stand, but hath an end. No man can enter into a strong man's house, and spoil his goods, except he will first bind the strong man; and then he will spoil his house.*

When you are in the Kingdom of God, all you have to do is become, receive, walk in it, and proclaim it. It is already yours. The Kingdom has made provision. No stronghold can stay in your life because provision can only come when the strong man is already bound up. Receive the finished work of Christ.

The Kingdom and the Church

I am trying to get you to see that being saved (being a Kingdom citizen) is not just about going to a building. The Church is not just a building where people gather; it is the educational epicenter of the Kingdom. It is where you come to learn and be empowered to do, not sit. The Kingdom is about doing, not just hearing. You must be a doer of the Word in order to see it activated in your life (James 1:23).

I hear people say all the time, "That's for when I get to heaven." No, you are seated in heavenly places already. Where you are now came from heaven. He brought the Kingdom with Him. You are seated in heavenly places.

Adam and the Blessing

Here is a powerful Kingdom key in Genesis 2:4 (from a Kingdom perspective):

> **Genesis 2:4-5** – *"These are the generation of Heaven, of the earth, when they were created in the day that the Lord God made the earth and heavens. Every plant of the field before it was in the earth and every herb of the field before it grew, for the Lord God had not caused it to rain upon the earth, and there was not (or because there was not) a man to till the ground."*

When I was studying this in one of the Jewish commentaries, it said that when God created the earth, He created all the trees, all the plant life, but they did not grow—all the trees were just beneath the soil. All the seeds were ready to come forth, but there was no man. So, He caused a mist to go over the earth to preserve the seed.

The Jewish communities teach that the earth waited for Adam. They claim it was Adam's job to speak to what was beneath the soil and command it to come forth to the surface. It was not in the sight realm. It was in the invisible realm, but it was there, waiting for his commandment. The Bible says in Genesis 2:

> **Genesis 2:6-8, 15** (NKJV) – *There went up a mist from the earth and watered the whole face of the ground. And the Lord God formed the man of the dust of the ground and breathed into his nostril the breath of life, and man became a living being. And the Lord God*

planted a Garden, eastward of Eden, and there he put the man whom he had formed... And the Lord God took the man and put him in the Garden of Eden to dress it and to keep it.

Now, when they say, "to dress it," this means to speak and to "keep it." This speaks of obedience. God did not create man in the Garden. He created man outside the Garden and put him inside it.

Now if the entire earth were completely gardened, if I may say, "gardened," then there would be no need to create a garden and put man there. The entire earth did not look like a garden. And so, man was created outside the beauty of the Garden and saw what life outside of the Garden (the Kingdom) looked like and had the desire to make the entire earth look like the Garden (the Kingdom), the place he was created to live in.

It is outside the Garden that God spoke to Adam and said, "Be fruitful and multiply." He was not just talking about having children. That was not the issue. That's the elementary version of it.

The Kingdom version is: "Adam, I have created this Garden. I have placed you in it. You have seen the condition outside of the Garden. I need you to use your God-image that I've created you in and begin to multiply this Garden throughout the earth."

The question is: are you multiplying the Kingdom?

The Garden provided everything they needed to live a full and happy life on the earth. Outside the Garden was lack and toil. One of the first things God did to Adam in the Garden was decree Adam to be blessed! Matthew 5 in the Amplified Bible defines "blessed" as "happy, to be envied, and spiritually prosperous, with life, joy and satisfaction in God's favor and salvation, regardless of outward condition." That means Adam was so empowered by God that outside conditions could not shake his joy. He was empowered to influence the environment and not be influenced by it!

> **Genesis 1:27-28** (AMP) – *So God created man in His own image, in the image and likeness of God He created him; male and female He created them. And God blessed them and said to them, Be fruitful, multiply, and fill the earth, and subdue it [using all its vast resources in the service of God and man]; and have dominion over the fish of the sea, the birds of the air, and over every living creature that moves upon the earth.*

This blessing allowed him to function in his Kingdom purpose, without interruption. The blessing was strong on Adam's life. The curse that was handed down on him because of his disobedience could not be active while he was still in the Garden.

> **Genesis 3:23-24** (AMP) – *Therefore the Lord God sent him forth from the Garden of Eden to till the ground from which he was taken. So [God] drove out the man; and He placed at the east of the Garden of Eden the cherubim and a flaming sword which turned every way, to keep and guard the way to the tree of life.*

God had to drive Adam out of the Garden in order for the curse to begin. Adam did not want to leave the place of perfect provision. He did not want to leave the environment that was voice activated. There was no toiling (hard labor) there. Adam just spoke what he desired and it happened. The earth had no choice but to obey him. It recognized its lord.

Once outside the Garden, the Bible says that Adam lived to be over 900 years old. I believe that it took death that long to figure out how to bring Adam back down to the earth in which he came from (which was part of his punishment).

When Adam was expelled from the Garden, he was expelled from the Kingdom of God. That's why the coming of Christ was so profound. He not only came to die for man's sin, but to empower and reinstate the authority that man once had in the earth. This allows you to be fruitful and multiply. You bring the Kingdom everywhere you go. You should be just as anointed at work as you are when you sing on the praise and worship team at church.

Satan's mission is to frustrate you and to drive you out of the territory he once ruled. Your assignment is to replace anything that represents or even looks like the old ruler-ship (the kingdom of darkness). Christ has assured you, through His word that, as long as you stay operating in the laws of the Kingdom and operating in the image that God created you in, things will always work.

If we can become who God has created us to be, then what you will be able to accomplish in one year will surpass what you've done for the last 10-15 years of your life. There are no weak citizens in the Kingdom of God. We don't beg. We don't pout. We always speak from a position of power. Speak that your business is increasing, that your family is saved, and that your ministry is exploding.

When you step into purpose, it may be the loneliest spot you've ever stepped into. Christ had massive crowds following Him until it was time to fulfill His reason for coming—dying for the sins of the world. When He really stepped into purpose, that's when He found Himself by Himself.

People will follow you all the way up until its time to do that thing that God has called you to do—by yourself. That's when separation from everyone else that has nothing to do with your assignment begins to happen.

End of Chapter Prayer

Father, we praise you for the anointing and calling us to be caretakers of the earth and have dominion over it. We come against fear, doubt, and unbelief for those are foreign to us. We were not created to have fear, doubt, unbelief, worry, sickness, hatred, envy, or jealousy operating in our lives. Our bodies were not created to fornicate. We receive the blessing that comes with operating the principles of Your Kingdom.

Father, we thank you that you made everything new when we came into the Kingdom. I pray that you surround your people with those who can propel them to their next place in destiny.

I blow away all the bloodsuckers of their destiny. I pray that their eyes will open and see who is really for them and who is against them. I pray that the hand of God will be upon them like never before.

I pray that the Holy Ghost in them will challenge them to rise up out of mediocrity, to think larger than they have ever thought before, to be bigger than they have ever been before, to dream beyond their natural means. I pray You'll begin to give them Kingdom understanding. Let the Kingdom become their obsession, like it has become mine. For You said, "Seek ye first the Kingdom, and all these things will be added," in Jesus' name we pray.

Kingdom Living Nuggets

- Man was created outside the beauty of the Garden and saw what life outside the Garden (the Kingdom) looked like.
- The Garden was a place of full provision to live a full life in the earth.
- The blessing allows you to function in His Kingdom purpose, without interruptions.
- When Adam was expelled from the Garden, he had lost the Kingdom.
- Satan's mission is to frustrate you and drive you out of the territory he once ruled.
- When you step into purpose, it may be the loneliest spot you've ever stepped into.
- People will follow you all the way up until its time to do the thing God has called you to do—by yourself.

Chapter 9

The Church in the Wilderness

According to Acts 7:38 (KJV) "This is he, that was in the Church in the wilderness" What is the Church in the Wilderness? The Church in the Wilderness is the Church that has provision without possession.

The truth is many Christians are living this way. While we have things provided for our needs—the bills get paid, the rent gets paid—you live without possessing. Living a life where your rent gets paid until next month but then you need to believe and trust God for the following month's rent is not living the abundant life. The abundant life is ownership and possession.

Unfortunately, there are those in the body of Christ who have become quite professional at living a Church in the Wilderness life. Make it your goal and focus not to get comfortable in mediocrity. God made you a citizen of the Kingdom. You're ambassadors. God wants you to live a victorious life not some of the time but all the time

(Deut 28:13). This is your time to possess everything that God has predestined for you (Rom 8:28-30).

How to Possess Your Territory

Possession is a part of the Kingdom mandate. Joshua is known as the book of conquests. The book of Joshua gives us three stages of possession. Why are these steps important? These are the steps:

1. **Enter the land/System.**
2. **Conquer the land/System.**
3. **Possess the land/System.**

There is a clear difference between all three steps of the process. It's the confusion of this process that has tangled up and frustrated so many Christians in the body of Christ. You're about to understand why the Bible says we are *more than conquerors* (Romans 8:37). Conquering is not the end of the battle.

Let's take a look at some definitions that will help us understand and apply these steps to make them a part of our Kingdom mandate. The word *"conquer"* means to acquire by force or arms, to overcome by force, or to subdue. *"Possessed"* means to occupy, to dominate, or to control from within. A secular dictionary gave an example of the word "possess" as a person that is demon possessed. They are being controlled from within.

The second definition of "possessed" was to make owner or master. And so to conquer speaks of the step that precedes you becoming a possessor. You must conquer before you can possess. To say that you conquer something means that you used force to subdue it. However, for me to possess the land, means I control what I have subdued.

Christ worked all three of the possessing principles. First, He had to make entry into the earth. He first entered through the Word. John and the prophets before him spoke for hundreds, even thousands of years to prepare for Jesus' coming. He then came through Mary, stayed here 30 years undetected—nobody really knew who He was—learning our ways, and then, when He began to cast out demons and devils, He started His conquest.

He was taking over by force. He started casting out devils, opening blind eyes, unstopping deaf ears, causing lame people to walk, and resurrecting the dead. That was Christ conquering. Note what He said in Luke 10:19 (AMP), "Behold! I have given you authority and power to trample upon serpents and scorpions, and [physical and mental strength and ability] over all the power that the enemy [possesses]; and nothing shall in any way harm you." That statement shows a person who has grasped possession. Why? You can't give away what you don't possess. From a Kingdom perspective, we know that the earth belongs to us (Psalms 115:16). Adam lost his rights through disobedience, but through Christ, we are empowered to take back what was created for us.

Joshua 1:11 (KJV) – *"Pass through the host and command the people saying, 'Prepare you victuals, for within three days, you shall pass over this Jordan to go in to possess the land.'"*

He didn't say, "You shall pass over this Jordan and possess the land." He said, "You shall pass over this Jordan *to go in*, to possess the land." I really need you to understand the distinction. Many of us have entered into an environment, but have not gained control of the environment. There's a difference. If the enemy can blur the distinction on entering versus possessing, then he's got us thinking we have the victory when he's still in control of the environment. Entry into a territory is just the first step. There are areas of business, music, or politics that God has opened the door to us, but the open door is just the beginning. Now that you're in the environment, you must take it over by force by using the tools God has given you through the Holy Spirit and the Kingdom.

It is not enough for you just to be standing on the territory. You must conquer the territory you entered, implementing Kingdom laws, which will in turn produce its way of living in that environment. All through the bible God constantly empowered warriors, like David and Joshua, to enter and conquer. These strategies were to become a pattern of possession, to the New Testament church, to learn from and apply in our respective fields of influence.

In order to appreciate this process, we must first appreciate the wisdom of God. When you as a believer are in an environment, you give Him (God) entry. Then He allows you to see things that you can conquer through prayer in the Spirit. It then becomes your job to possess the territory, in which you now have influence, from the inside. You create policy. You say what goes on the TV that feeds the minds of our young. You decide whether our kids learn about Creationism or Darwinism. That's possession.

This is true in every sphere of life. This is the formula that has been given to us to possess territory. Once you make up your mind to fulfill your Kingdom assignment, there are blessings that will fall upon your life.

> **Exodus 23: 20-23, 25** (KJV) – *"Behold, I sent an angel before you to keep you and to guard you along the way, and to bring you to the place which I have prepared unto you. Give heed to him, listen to him, obey him. But if you do not listen to him and obey his voice that I speak, I will put an enemy to your*

enemies. You shall serve the Lord your God, he shall bless your bread and your water, and I will take sickness from the midst of you. None shall lose her young by miscarriage or the barren in your land. I will fulfill the number of your days."

God had given Israel an angel to guide and lead them just like God has given us the Holy Spirit. The Holy Spirit guides us and leads us into all truth.

When you get in the mindset of possession, you will discover that there are promises attached to possess. If you get stuck in an "I'm just a worker" mentality, you will always be in provision mode, but never have possession.

If you're more than a conqueror, what are you? You're a possessor. You just don't conquer, you possess. You own. You take territory. You take realms. You take spheres. You take businesses. You take houses. You are a possessor, not just a conqueror. That's the Kingdom mindset.

Nehemiah 9:36-38 (KJV) – *Behold, we are servants this day, and for the land that thou gavest unto our fathers to eat the fruit thereof and the good thereof, behold, we are servants in it: And it yielded much increase unto the kings whom thou hast set over us because of our sins: also they have dominion over our bodies, and over our cattle, at their pleasure, and we are in great distress. And because of all this we make a sure covenant, and write it; and our princes, Levites, and priests, seal unto it.*

This Scripture makes it very clear that because of our lack of movement and obedience to the Kingdom mandate, the world's systems have dominion over everything that belongs to us—and that puts us in distress. So, we cannot feel comfortable. If we feel comfortable being beneath, instead of above, something's wrong.

Those in the ninth chapter of Nehemiah knew they were living contrary to how they were created and that caused them to want a new covenant. They knew they were not designed to be slaves to the world's system, but a liberator of it. They awoke to the fact that someone else was enjoying their inheritance.

Nehemiah 9:19-22 (KJV) – *Yet though in thy manifold mercies forsookest them not in the wilderness. The pillar of cloud departed not from them by day, to lead them in the way, neither the pillar of fire by night, to shew them light and the way wherein they should go. Yeah, 40 years didst thou sustain them in the wilderness so that they lacked nothing. Their clothes waxed not old, and their feet swelled not. Moreover, thou gavest us them kingdoms and nations.*

God not only preserved them, He also gave them kingdoms and nations. This is what God did for them in their obedient state. If this was done for them—and they didn't have Christ, just the law of the Old Testament, and you're a new creature in Christ Jesus—how much more will He do for you?

Know that He's given you kingdoms and dominion. He commissioned the disciples to disciple nations (Matt 29:19).

Where There Is Possession, There Will Be Provision

Be assured; there can be provision without possession, but there will never be possession (in the Kingdom) without provision. This was the case with the people of Israel in Egypt.

Deuteronomy 11:8-12 (AMP) – *Therefore you shall keep all the commandments which I command you today, that you may be strong and go in and possess the land which you go across [the Jordan] to possess, And that you may live long in the land which the Lord swore to your fathers to give to them and to their descendants, a land flowing with milk and honey. For the land which you go in to possess is not like the land of Egypt, from which you came out, where you sowed your seed and watered it with your foot laboriously as in a garden of vegetables. But the land which you enter to possess is a land of hills and valleys which drinks water of the rain of the heavens,*

When the people of Israel were in Egypt, they worked to get provision, but they still did not possess the land. God was giving them territory that they would not only have provision but also possession. That's Kingdom!

In everything Joshua did, all the territory he possessed, and every time he possessed territory, there was always provision where there was possession (gold and silver, which represented wealth). They didn't have to struggle. Wealth was transferred to them with the territory. Solomon possessed in one year— his annual income—$325 million from one source of income. That's Kingdom wealth.

Stop settling for crumbs when God has given you the whole land. Stop settling for a block when He has given you the city. For it is not enough just to conquer, but you must possess. That is the Kingdom mentality. That is the Kingdom perspective. God can increase you so much until you'll not only have enough to be a blessing to others but also to leave an inheritance for your children's children (Prov 13:22).

Solomon had so much wealth that he had one department where they counted his money 24 hours, 7 days a week. All they did was count his wealth. It's time for the Kingdom wealth transfer through possession!

Kingdom Living Nuggets

- You are in the wilderness, if you have provision without possession.
- Possession is a part of the Kingdom mandate.
- Once you make up your mind to do your Kingdom assignment, there are blessings that will fall upon your life.
- If you are more than a conqueror, what are you? You're a possessor.
- Due to the Church's lack of movement toward the Kingdom mandate, the world's systems have dominion over everything that belongs to us—and that has put us in distress.
- Every territory Joshua possessed always came with provision
- Know that He's given you kingdoms and dominion
- Stop settling for crumbs when God has given you the whole land
- You're not just a conqueror but a possessor.
- It's time for the Kingdom wealth transfer through possession!

Chapter 10

Lessons from Kingdom Parables

The Wheat and Tares

The stalks of the wheat and tares must grow together.

Matthew 13: 37-43 (KJV) - *He answered and said unto them, He that soweth the good seed is the Son of man; The field is the world; the good seed are the children of the kingdom; but the tares are the children of the wicked one; The enemy that sowed them is the devil; the harvest is the end of the world; and the reapers are the angels. As therefore the tares are gathered and burned in the fire; so shall it be in the end of this world. The Son of man shall send forth his angels, and they shall gather out of his kingdom all things that offend, and them which do iniquity; And shall cast them into a furnace of fire: there shall be wailing and gnashing of teeth. Then shall the righteous shine forth as the sun in the kingdom of their Father. Who hath ears to hear, let him hear.*

This parable is not speaking of members within the church. When we speak of the Kingdom of God, the Scripture above is referring to what the enemy did while we slept—ignoring our purpose. The enemy sent tares into our lives. While we, the church, were busy being religious, the enemy was rising up politicians to tell us what to do and what our kids should be learning in school. Laws are changing. Society is shifting. And the enemy is strategically placing people in controlling and financial positions of these movements.

The unique thing about tares is that they look almost identical to wheat. The untrained eye would never be able to distinguish the difference. I believe that's why the Bible says we shall know one another by the fruit we produce (Matt 7:20). In other words, are your actions producing Kingdom results?

It is time for the body of Christ to get up, get out, and possess the land. Go and possess the earth. Let God use you to take over territories—industries, businesses, and so forth. The enemy strategizes on how to possess the territory that God gave to us to make sure that His people get into the right spots to promote His agenda.

Right now, during the writing of this book, New York has passed a law legalizing same sex marriage. One of the things that I have found very interesting is the strategy of the gay agenda. The following is from the Wall Street Journal (Gay Marriage Vote In 6/25/11):

> *"Since their loss in 2009, gay activist raised money to help unseat three lawmakers opposed to gay marriage and replace them with senators who pledged their support for the bill.*
>
> *"Ultimately, Republican concerns were outweighed by pressure from Mr. Cuomo, who lent his muscle to a disciplined, multimillion dollar advocacy campaign waged by national and local gay-rights leaders.*

"Instead of trying to defeat Senate Republicans and prop up their adversaries, gay-rights activist wooed them with a blend of courtship and threats that gradually wore down their resistance."

Unfortunately, the body of Christ has become reactive instead of proactive, and that must change. Only after certain politicians' rise to power do we want to call a fast and pray them out. Let God use your gift to show you what He is doing and to let God give you a plan to counter the attack. That is the true power of the Kingdom. As citizens of the Kingdom of God, we do not vote party or color, but we vote according to the laws of the Kingdom. The Kingdom is our political party. We align our political agenda and choose candidates based upon the Biblical principles of God.

God did not just pray from heaven when He realized what the enemy had done to the earth. He had to have a plan and a strategy to counter. He sent His Son. His Son had to come, to be beaten, to die, and to be resurrected in order to get the results God wanted and give the Kingdom back to the people of God.

I believe wholeheartedly that I am a man of prayer, but after I pray, there must be action. Something in the earth has to say that I've been in the presence of God. In the Old Testament, God gave specific instructions on how to win battles, and He will do the same for you. We can pray for people to get saved all day, but at some point, someone must go and tell them about Jesus in order to see the results of that prayer.

The Net of the Kingdom

Matthew 13: 47-50 (KJV) – *"Again the Kingdom of heaven is like a net that was cast into the sea and gathered of every kind, which when it was full drew into shore and set down and gathered the good into the vessels, but cast the bad away. So shall it be at the end of the world, when the angels shall come forth and sever the wicked from among the just and shall cast them into the furnace of fire. There shall be wailing and gnashing of teeth."*

In this parable, the Kingdom represents the entire earth and our ability to dominate the earth. There are those who are caught up in the net who are not believers. Therefore, there are laws and principles that are designed to work in the earth whether you're a believer or not.

You may wonder how a person has grown to a great level of wealth. Most likely, they are using certain principles to govern their lives. A principle is a principle. A law is a law—regardless of whether you are black, white, green, or yellow. If you run a red light, you are guilty of breaking the law. The law makes no distinction between race, color, or creed. There are certain laws and principles that govern our lives, regardless of whether we are saved or unsaved. Principles work if you apply them.

But, according to the Bible, what matters is at the end. After this is all over, what separates you from everybody else is the fact that they are going to be cast into hell and you are going to inherit the earth. He says, "So don't be intimidated." David said, "I almost slipped; when I saw the prosperity of the wicked" (Psalms 73:2-3, KJV).

Never envy another's supposed success. It is one thing to have money, but true prosperity isn't only material wealth. It is also peace, joy, and love.

Go and possess what God has given you the authority to possess. If you use these laws, principles, and methods of operation, then God will begin to expand your territory, expand your business, and expand your ability to influence. The earth belongs to you. So, when you give, you give with purpose, knowing you are giving it because you have power and authority over all creation.

Once you become saved, the renewing of your mind is crucial. This renewed mindset helps you to see and receive God's best for your life. Complaining and murmuring causes your workplace or your place of living to become a wilderness, and you get stuck there. Why stay in a wilderness when God has something better for you? Because you have created that wilderness through your confession, you must dismantle it through your confession.

The Mustard Seed

> **Matthew 13:31-32** (KJV) – *"Another parable put he forth unto them, saying, 'The Kingdom of heaven is like to a grain of mustard seed, which a man took and sowed in his field, which indeed is the least of all seeds, but when it is grown, it is the greatest among herbs and becometh a tree, so that the birds of the air come and lodge in the branches thereof."*

This is a very powerful parable. He explains that the Kingdom of God is like a seed, which is extremely small in size. But in due time, it's supposed to grow, and then it takes over the area in which it was initially undetected. Here God gives us another *Kingdom strategy*.

If you are in the Kingdom of God—the Kingdom, the Bible says, is within you—then whatever you do is seed. You may, at times, find yourself asking, "God, why am I here at this job?" It is because you are a seed. You might even ask, "Why am I living in this part of the world?" It is simply because you are a seed. Why does God have you in government, law, or education? It is simple, you are a seed. As we all know, the mustard seed is one of the smallest seeds in existence today. It speaks symbolically of God planting His people undetected. I like how Lance Wallnau—a great Kingdom teacher—says it: "God will do a covert operation."

He needs to plant you in that place and then allow the Word to grow in you, in that area, until people come to you to ask questions and direction. Metaphorically, we as Kingdom citizens are like a tree that provides nourishment for a variety of creatures. The birds that lodge in your tree are the people attaching themselves to you and saying, "How are you so successful at what you do? How are you so talented?" These questions become your opportunity to say, "Well, let me tell you about the source of my wisdom. Let me tell you about the source of my knowledge. Let me tell you who my teacher is—the greatest teacher on the face of the earth, God." Now you become more of a witness for the Kingdom.

Kingdom Living Nuggets

- The unique thing about tares is that they look almost identical to wheat
- After prayer, there must be action.
- Let God use your gift to show you what He is doing and give you a plan to counter the attack.
- Whatever you do is a seed
- Once you become saved, the renewing of your mind is crucial
- Complaining and murmuring causes your workplace to become a wilderness
- Principles work if you apply them
- We can pray for people to get saved all day, but at some point, someone must go and tell them about Jesus
- Kingdom citizens are like a tree that provides nourishment for a variety of creatures

PART 4:
Spread the Garden

Chapter 11

You Are the Solution

There are many great men and women of God who were great examples of this principle in action. Sometimes you can't pull out the oil and the prayer shawl, but your life is still a living epistle (2 Corinthians 3:3).

The Bible says Christ exalted his Word above His name.

Psalms 138:2 (KJV) – *I will worship toward Your holy temple and praise Your name for Your loving-kindness and for Your truth and faithfulness; for You have **exalted** above all else Your name and Your **word** and You have magnified Your **word** above all Your name.*

That means, if you live in a country where you can't publicly say the name of Jesus, that may be your faith has not built up to the place of boldness like Peter or Paul's. If, however, you live the lifestyle and principles of the Word, which Christ has exalted above His name, you will get the same results! When you are in the Kingdom, God never promotes you for the sole purpose of more money. Although we know that the blessing of prosperity is included by default. If we walk according to God's Word and plan, God promotes us for the purpose of giving us more visibility and influence. Before Christ left the earth, He gave the disciples visibility.

When your heart is right, God through the power of "The Blessing" (Deuteronomy 28) will promote you quickly within your industry. God continues to elevate you, because the higher you go, the more people you can influence.

I will never forget an experience I had. A woman come up to me and informed me that her employer prohibited her from reading her Bible at lunch. She said, "Is that legal?" I said, "Of course that's not legal. You know, you can fight that, but don't take it too personal and don't leave." She was ready to pack up and leave her job. I said, "Don't leave. The opposition means they really need you there." Remember that the enemy comes to bring opposition. Don't leave a location because trouble comes. Remember, you are a seed.

At times, the warfare you feel at your job is because of the change you are about to bring. When the enemy gets a whiff that you are about to influence an area or bring a change, he is going to try and frustrate you in order to get you out of the place God has called you to conquer. God has strategically placed you in the midst of a problem to represent the Kingdom and its laws as the solution.

How does promotion come to you? Biblically, a promotion comes with your ability to solve a problem. And so—watch this—Daniel was promoted from the dungeon to be the king's right-hand man all because he was able to interpret—provide a solution to—a problem. As his gifts and ability kicked in, God gave him the ability to do the work. He received a promotion.

Daniel 2:1-2, 10-11, 16, 27-28, 46-48 (KJV) – *And in the second year of the reign of Nebuchadnezzar, Nebuchadnezzar dreamed dreams, wherewith his spirit was troubled, and his sleep brake from him. Then* *the king commanded to call the magicians, and the astrologers, and the sorcerers, and the Chaldeans, for to shew the king his dreams. So they came and stood before the king.*

The Chaldeans answered before the king, and said, There is not a man upon the earth that can shew the king's matter: therefore there is no king, lord, nor ruler, that asked such things at any magician, or astrologer, or Chaldean. And it is a rare thing that the king requireth, and there is none other that can shew it before the king, except the gods, whose dwelling is not with flesh.

Then Daniel went in, and desired of the king that he would give him time, and that he would shew the king the interpretation.

Daniel answered in the presence of the king, and said, The secret which the king hath demanded cannot the wise men, the astrologers, the magicians, the soothsayers, shew unto the king; But there is a God in heaven that revealeth secrets, and maketh known to the king Nebuchadnezzar what shall be in the latter days. Thy dream, and the visions of thy head upon thy bed, are these;

Then the king Nebuchadnezzar fell upon his face, and worshipped Daniel, and commanded that they should offer an oblation and sweet odours unto him. The king answered unto Daniel, and said, Of a truth it is, that your God is a God of gods, and a Lord of kings, and a revealer of secrets, seeing thou couldest reveal this secret. Then the king made Daniel a great man, and gave him many great gifts, and made him ruler over the whole province of Babylon, and chief of the governors over all the wise men of Babylon.

God will anoint you to first identify the problem and, secondly, to solve the problem. Why? Promotion increases influence. Daniel's gift made room for him to properly represent the Kingdom in his government. If there are governmental issues that bother you, maybe it is your assignment! Notice that, as a result of Daniel becoming a solution first, the king adorned him with wealth (Daniel 2:29). The wealth became a byproduct of him being in a certain position. Many of us are trying to become wealthy outside our position of influence when wealth and provision are eagerly awaiting us next to the solution.

Not only did Daniel receive a promotion, but because he was promoted to a position of power and influence, he was also able to promote his three Hebrew friends to a place of influence by using the same Kingdom formula.

Daniel 2:49 (KJV) – *Then Daniel requested of the king, and he set Shadrach, Meshach, and Abednego, over the affairs of the province of Babylon: but Daniel sat in the gate of the king.*

All through the Bible, promotion comes with your ability to solve a problem. That is amazing! That is what the Kingdom is supposed to do—put other Kingdom influencers in positions of authority.

Joseph was another powerful example of solutions leading to promotion. Pharaoh had a dream and no one could interpret it. Let me stop here for a second and say that God will frustrate the dreams of leaders, CEOs, and managers until you come along. The Kingdom is anointed to interpret and provide answers to problems, because the one that can interpret it is usually the one who carries it out. It is one thing to dream it, but it is another to interpret—carry out and execute—what has been dreamed.

Once Joseph interpreted the dream, the king promoted Joseph.

Genesis 41:37-44 (KJV) – *And the thing was good in the eyes of Pharaoh, and in the eyes of all his servants. And Pharaoh said unto his servants, Can we find such a one as this is, a man in whom the Spirit of God is? And Pharaoh said unto Joseph, Forasmuch as God hath shewed thee all this, there is none so discreet and wise as thou art: Thou shalt be over my house, and according unto thy word shall all my people be ruled: only in the throne will I be greater than thou. And Pharaoh said unto Joseph, See, I have set thee over all the land of Egypt. And Pharaoh took off his ring from his hand, and put it upon Joseph's hand, and arrayed him in vestures of fine linen, and put a gold chain about his neck; And he made him to ride in the second chariot which he had; and they cried before him, Bow the knee: and he made him ruler over all the land of Egypt. And Pharaoh said unto Joseph, I am Pharaoh, and without thee shall no man lift up his hand or foot in all the land of Egypt.*

Joseph became so influential that he set up the first commodities exchange market during a famine. The Bible says the whole world came to buy and sell from Egypt. Why is this powerful? Because much later in Scripture, the Egyptians would hand over their wealth to the Israelites as they left to go to the Promised Land. This would have never been possible if Joseph had not been placed in a position of power and influence years before.

If there are issues in the workplace that you are not happy with, and you have a better idea, stop complaining and solve the problem. Your ability to solve a problem positions you to give God the credit for your success.

Chapter Prayer

God, I pray that every citizen of the Kingdom will become uncomfortable being less than who You've called him or her to be. Give them strength, ability, and wisdom. Show them problems and then give them the solutions. Give them the avenue to show forth the solution that it may be implemented.

I come against every force of the enemy that would try to come and steal the glory from the Kingdom of God where the solution was applied. We come against strategies of the devil, strategies against our families, strategies against our children, strategies against our home and our finances. We break free from the system of financial struggle. We break free from the system of sickness.

We exercise our power over creation, and we command resources to come to us now in the name of Jesus. We command opportunities to come to us now. Make us people of purpose, not just churchgoers, but citizens. Amen.

Kingdom Living Nuggets

- While the Church was busy being religious, the enemy was raising up politicians to tell us what to do and what our children should be learning in school.
- Let God use you to take over territories and industries.
- As Kingdom citizens, we do not vote party or color, but we vote according to the laws of the Kingdom in which we serve.
- You must be a person of prayer, but after you pray, there must be action.
- Once you accept Christ into your life, the renewing of your mind is crucial.
- God has strategically placed you in the midst of a problem to represent the Kingdom and its laws as the solution.
- God will anoint you first to identify the problem and, secondly, to solve the problem by being a lasting solution.

Chapter 12

The Kingdom Is Not to Hold

Remember, the working definition for "dominion" is to govern, rule, control, manage, lead, affect, and impact. When the Word says, "I've given you dominion over the earth," He's saying, "I've given you the power to govern, to rule, to control, to manage, to lead, to affect, and to impact." These are the seven aspects of having dominion.

- Govern
- Rule
- Control
- Manage
- Lead
- Affect
- Impact

When you come into the full understanding of living a life of dominion, these seven facets will change your life.

There will obviously be times in life where you cannot control situations, but you can control how you allow them to affect you. Unfortunately, sometimes we allow other people's actions to affect us. Though you cannot control all aspects of other people's actions and the resulting consequences, a Kingdom person, through the Word, can control how they react to these situations.

In the Kingdom, we understand that we do not have to allow situations to pull us out of character. Our authority and our posture must be one of: "I am in control, and the enemy does not control this situation." Understanding who you are in the Kingdom is imperative.

Daniel 2:44 expresses the ultimate plan of God when it comes to the Kingdom.

Daniel 2:44 (KJV) – *And in the days of these kings, the final ten kings, shall the God of Heaven set up a Kingdom, which shall never be destroyed, nor shall its sovereignty be left to another people, but it shall break and crush and consume all these kingdoms, and it shall stand forever.*

God's ultimate agenda is to set up a Kingdom that will reign supreme above all other kingdoms. In the end, only His Kingdom will stand. Thank you, Jesus!

The Bible says, "We are destroyed for the lack of knowledge" (Hosea 4:6). Knowledge does not need to be revealed to us. It is information that has been made available to us already. The problem is we have rejected it and have thus destroyed ourselves. In previous chapters, I've shown you that you were built for the Kingdom of God. In you resides the Kingdom principles and the Kingdom laws.

It's time to wear the Kingdom like a fragrance. There's so much power and glory on the inside of you that wherever you go, people are going to want to bless you, and doors are going to open, because you're walking in the favor of the Kingdom.

Jesus told His disciples, "You've seen me operate in the power of the Kingdom. I give you the power" (Luke 10:19). He imparts Kingdom power into the twelve, and the twelve went out and began spreading the Kingdom. Here's the principle: the Kingdom is not given to hold, but to give. The Kingdom cannot work where there is selfishness. Love is the foundation of the Kingdom.

The Church will never be able to take over the world's systems until we begin to allow the Kingdom message to be multiplied. Prior to Jesus releasing the twelve to spread the Kingdom, Jesus did not receive much attention from those in the governmental circles. But when He began to multiply Himself, He received the attention of Herod and the Roman government. The government took note when the movement was no longer just one man. Now there were twelve. Those twelve started multiplying themselves and so on. This is Kingdom multiplication.

The Bible says, "The enemy comes immediately" (Mark 4:15). Scripture begins to take on new meaning when you understand this. The enemy doesn't want the Word to grow. Why? Because he knows that if the Word of God ever takes root in your life and becomes the new core basis for your decision making process, the Word will begin to multiply. Make it your business to multiply the power of God. Don't have one moment of dead space.

Righteousness in the Kingdom

You reign as kings in life. You are a king. Kings represent the status of all power and authority in this earthly realm.

Romans 5:18-20 (AMP) – *Well then, as one man's trespass, one man's false step and falling away led to condemnation for all men, so one man's act of* *righteousness leads to acquittal and right standing with God, and life for all men. For just as by one man's disobedience, failing to hear, heedlessly and carelessness, the many were constituted sinners, so by one man's disobedience, the many will be constituted righteous, made acceptable to God, brought into right standing with him. But then law came in, only to expand and increase the trespass, making it more apparent and exciting opposition. But where sin increased and abounded, grace, which is God's unmerited favor, has surpassed it and increased the more and super abound.*

Wherever sin was, grace was there in a much greater capacity. So whatever the strength of sin is in your life, it is nothing compared to the favor that God wants to give you when you step into righteousness. Favor towards you is a hundred times greater than the strength and the force of sin once you step over into righteousness.

You no longer operate in sin. You operate in the righteousness of God. I am not trying to become righteous. I am the righteousness of Christ. Just like you received salvation, you received righteousness. You don't work on becoming righteous, because you are righteous through Christ.

When you come into the Kingdom of God, from day one, God was always giving you prototypes of the Kingdom. God has been doing this since the time man fell.

When Abraham obeyed God, God counted his faith as righteousness. Because God saw him as righteousness, God gave him a promise that we (as believers) today are beneficiaries of. All through the Old Testament, we see God staying committed to His promise to the people that came out of the loins of Abraham. Why? Abraham was a righteous man.

Abraham was seen as righteous in the eyes of God, and God immediately began applying Kingdom principles to him. He told Abraham to leave where he was, and to travel to a land that He would give him.

1 Chronicles 20:1-7 (KJV) – *And it came to pass that after the year was expired, when kings go out to battle, Joab led forth the army and devastated the land of the Ammonites, and came and besieged Rabbah. But David tarried at Jerusalem. And Joab smote Rabbah, and destroyed it. David took the crown of their king from off his head, and found it to way a talent of gold, and there were precious stones in it; and it was set upon David's head: and he brought exceeding much spoil out of the city.*

Do you see the pattern? David is subduing territory. Anything in your life that is contrary to the Word of God (the Kingdom of God) is something you have a right to bring down. You don't have to tolerate the devil's mess. You have a right to bring it down and the power to slay every giant.

David was given the authority to slay every giant. However, God became displeased when David started counting his men. David didn't understand that battles were not won by natural resources, but by Kingdom resources.

You were saved to subdue kingdoms! You were saved to subdue territories! You were saved to subdue systems! David was empowered to conquer territory and all the spoil and the wealth that came with it. David gained so much spoil, that he was able to share it with the whole camp and be a blessing to others. David gave away gold, silver, and cattle. That's what the Kingdom does, positions you to be a conduit of the blessing.

When you come into the Kingdom of God, your days of slavery are over. Your days of pity parties are over. Your days of feeling sorry for yourself are over. It's time for you to rise up and become the person that God has destined you to become.

Praise Precedes Victory in the Kingdom

Praise is an important tool to win spiritual battles in the Kingdom.

> **2 Chronicles 20:25-28** (KJV) – *When Jehoshaphat and his people came to take the spoil, they found among them much cattle, goods, garments, precious things, which they took for themselves. And then they could carry away so much, that it took three days to gather all the spoil. They came to Jerusalem with harps, lyres and trumpets, to the house of God. And the fear of God came upon all the kingdom of those countries when they heard that the Lord had fought against the enemy of Israel.*

When other kingdoms (world systems and demonic influences) heard how God gave Israel the victory, they became fearful. In fact, God gave them a victory that forced the enemy to leave everything else they had. That's Kingdom living! As a result of this supernatural victory, the entire realm of Jehoshaphat was quiet, for his God gave him peace and rest round about him. When you live according to the principles of the Kingdom, the effects of the Word will cause your territory to become quiet.

Now hear this. This is phenomenal. How did Jehoshaphat get to the point where they were able to collect so much wealth that it took three days for a whole army to carry it? He gives us the answer in verse 21 (KJV): *"And when he had consulted with the people, he appointed singers to sing to the Lord, and praise him in their holy garments as they went out before the army, singing, 'Give thanks to the Lord, for his mercy and loving kindness endures forever.' And when they began to sing and to praise the Lord, he set ambush against the men of Ammon, Moab, Mount Seir, who had come against Judah, and they were self-slaughtered."*

Their praise preceded the victory. The enemy wants you to complain and murmur, because when you do, you strengthen his position in your life. However, he can't tolerate or win against the sound of praise. Praise wins battles, praise releases angels, and praise is a Kingdom weapon.

Kingdom Living Nuggets

- Never allow people or situations to pull you out of character.
- God's ultimate agenda is to set up a Kingdom that will reign and crush all other kingdoms.
- It's time to wear the Kingdom like a fragrance.
- The Kingdom is not given to us to hold, but to give. It cannot work where there is selfishness because love is its foundation.
- The church can never impact world systems until we begin to allow the Kingdom message to be multiplied.
- Whatever the strength of sin is in your life, it is nothing compared to the favor that God wants to give you when you step into righteousness.
- You were saved to subdue kingdoms! You were saved to subdue territories! You were saved to subdue systems!

CHAPTER 13

Kingdom House: A Kingdom Prototype

It was supposed to be only one year, but a year turned into four years. I was asked to begin a youth ministry at my church four years ago. My immediate response was, "NO!!!" I was too busy evangelizing and wanted to stay focused on that assignment. I was traveling at least once a week to another city and was sure this was all I was supposed to be doing.

Months went by, and I was approached again about starting a youth ministry in my church. Our church had been without a youth ministry for at least five years, and we were losing members who felt there was nothing there for their children. While I wanted to help, I saw no possible way to divide myself any further than I had already been divided, but I continued to put it in prayer. I did not want to take on an assignment only because I thought I could accomplish it, but I wanted to only do it if it was something God wanted me to do.

One morning, after wrestling with this decision, I picked up a local newspaper. On the front of the paper was a picture of a three year old dressed in gang colors and throwing up gang signs. I immediately thought of my three-year-old son at the time and said, "I don't want that kid on the same street as my son when they are teenagers." Before I could finish the thought, I heard the Spirit say, "So what are you going to do about it?" It was at that moment when I realized my assignment had been switched.

I contacted my leadership and committed only one year to getting the youth ministry up and running. Interestingly enough, it was at this time that I was receiving spiritual downloads from the Holy Spirit about the Kingdom revelation. I thought, *what better way to put the Kingdom principles to the test than to implement the principles within a youth ministry that was being built from scratch.* The youth ministry embodied this ideology and was named Kingdom House Youth Ministries (KHYM) where we would function solely on Kingdom principles.

My first assignment was to recruit and train twenty-five or more volunteer staff in the Kingdom principles. I immediately began teaching on the uniqueness of our assignment as a youth ministry and the ministry's ability to not only grow and bless our home church, but to bless the community and ultimately the world as well.

> **Acts 1:8** (KJV) - *But ye shall receive power, after that the Holy Ghost is come upon you: and ye shall be witnesses unto me both in Jerusalem, and in all Judaea, and in Samaria, and unto the uttermost part of the earth.*

Our mission and vision was developed at the onset and clearly illustrates how we sought to move in the direction of the Kingdom. Our mission and vision reads:

Kingdom House Vision Statement

Our Vision as a youth ministry is to facilitate a personal relationship between Christ and each young person, empowering this generation to affect their homes, neighborhoods, communities, and the world. We purpose to build youth who will excel spiritually, educationally, socially, and economically. It is our goal to provide an arena where youth of all cultures and nationalities can be developed, empowered and strategically aligned to fulfill their God-given purpose in shaping a Kingdom minded culture.

Kingdom House Mission Statement

Our Mission is to:

- *Provide youth with the tools necessary to discover and develop their God given identity and purpose*
- *Equip and empower youth through the word of God to overcome life's challenges*
- *Train each individual to maximize the great commission and make disciples*
- *Strategically direct each young person into Kingdom purpose*
- *Maximize cultural influence through Kingdom principles*

Remember, the Kingdom is about fulfilling the initial command that God gave Adam in the garden and using the power of "The Blessing" through the Holy Spirit, to fulfill that commission. Looking back, I realized one of my biggest challenges was shifting people's mindsets. The people of Israel were trapped in the wilderness, not due to lack of direction, but wrong thinking.

Numbers 13:29-33 (KJV) – *The Amalekites dwell in the land of the south: and the Hittites, and the Jebusites, and the Amorites, dwell in the mountains: and the Canaanites dwell by the sea, and by the coast of Jordan. And Caleb stilled the people before Moses, and said, Let us go up at once, and possess it; for we are well able to overcome it. But the men that went up with him said, We be not able to go up against the people; for they are stronger than we. And they brought up an evil report of the land which they had searched unto the children of Israel, saying, The land, through which we have gone to search it, is a land that eateth up the inhabitants thereof; and all the people that we saw in it are men of a great stature. And there we saw the giants, the sons of Anak, which come of the giants: and we were in our own sight as grasshoppers, and so we were in their sight.*

Joshua and Caleb's response came out of a renewed mind. They and the other spies all saw the same thing, but only they responded differently. The rest of the spies looked at the situation and forgot about what God had said. In Genesis, God saw darkness but spoke light. Once you become a believer, you must then renew your mind with God's Word.

As a leader, I believe in allowing people to work in their strengths while they work on their weaknesses. One thing God graced me with is an extremely smart, talented, young, and passionate staff. When I approached many of them about joining KHYM, they either said, "No," or "Um…I'm not sure." That was, of course, before I told them this would be like no other youth ministry on the planet! They had been so "churched" out (in the traditional sense) that they didn't want to hear about getting involved with a youth ministry where the average stay is two years or less.

To help the staff make the transition into the Kingdom mindset, I made it mandatory for my entire staff to read *Church Shift* by Sunday Adelija. Changing the mindsets of the staff was not easy, but with hard work, it was doable. Reading Pastor Sunday's *Church Shift,* helped the staff to think like a king and to think Kingdom.

I also became a stickler for structure, order, and accountability. I was, and still am, a strong believer in order. When God spoke to Moses about building the tabernacle, the glory of God did not enter until that last piece of furniture was put into place. Only when it was completed entirely did the glory of God fill the temple. Order is important.

We broke our youth into three groups: ABC (Abundantly Blessed Children Church) ages 2-6, Champions for God ages 7-12 and GIANTS (Generation Impacting a Nation to Surrender) ages 13-19. These groups would have weekly sessions that would help to empower each member with the Word of God. In addition to that, we started several programs that would serve those in KH and the community at large.

Part of thinking Kingdom was thinking about being the solution to someone's problem. So in response, we launched several programs that were designed to fit into one or more of the seven spheres of influence.

One of our most successful programs is called *Fashion House Academy* (FHA). FHA was downloaded into a young man, a real star, by the name of Ricardo—a.k.a. R. Stylr as we came to call him. He is a true pillar in the Kingdom House who also ran our GIANTS division. He was a professional stylist who had worked with companies such as Tommy Hilfiger and Fashion Week in New York City. I went to Rick and said, "We need a program to stick into the Arts and Entertainment mountain." Not too long after that, he came up with FHA.

FHA is an amazing program that allows potential young designers to design and make their own collection—yes, an entire collection—in less than a month and teaches students the fundamentals of character development. At the end of each session, they have a fashion gala where students have their clothing collection modeled by real models. We've even had models that had been featured on "Americas next Top Model" model our youth's clothing. FHA has had many news write ups and has been requested on numerous occasions to bring the program to multiple states. One of the things that made this such a Kingdom-minded program is the five core principles that each student had to learn from a biblical perspective. Those principles are determination, creativity, passion, character, and teamwork. We approached each of these five core values from a Kingdom perspective and have seen many young lives turned around for the Kingdom.

Another program is The Road to Higher Education (TRHE). TRHE was downloaded into another KH superstar by the name of Sadio. She is brilliant. She received her bachelor's degree in English and her master's degree in education and is passionate about inner city youth getting an education. TRHE was set up to enter the education mountain and combat the dropout rate in New York City. At that time, the dropout rate was very high. Sadio decided to use her already existing passion to be a solution.

TRHE was set up not only to combat the dropout rate, but also to expose inner city youth to careers and professions that they otherwise would have ever been exposed to. We've brought guests in to speak to our youth—a state judge and a city councilman to name a few—just for the purpose of exposure and to learn about the pathway to such influential career paths. At the end of the semester, each youth receives a road map that provided guidelines for reaching the career goal of their choice. This was very important to the students, because many of them came from broken homes and had no clear guidance as to how they could become that doctor or nurse they so desired to become.

Another program worth mentioning is Chefs R Us. This program has an influence in the Family Mountain of cultural influence. It was downloaded into a young lady with such a wonderful spirit by the name of Michelle. Chefs R Us on the surface looks like a cooking program for youth. However, the program focuses on rebuilding the family dynamic through family mealtime and conversation.

Those were just some of the tools that God gave us to reach youth in and outside of our church and expand the Kingdom. Many of our programs are about bringing the principles of the Kingdom into an environment. We've adopted entire schools and libraries. The earth moans and groans for us to come out of hiding and bring them solutions. The world needs your solutions.

While we are also excited about creating programs that have a great impact on society for the Kingdom, anyone that's ever brought a program to the social market knows that it's a lot of work. Making it successful is even more work. That is why I thank God for a young man that is a true gem in KHYM by the name of Kareem. Kareem is by far one of the brightest guys I know. We nicknamed him Mr. Economics. He has an amazing gift of understanding and creating complex models that increase the processes of any business, whether not-for-profit or for profit. Right out of high school, he received a full academic scholarship to New York's well-known New York University. His goal is to build complex economic models to solve extremely complex issues on behalf of the Kingdom. Now that's Kingdom!

Are You Ready for an Extreme Degree of a God Encounter?

Before I close this chapter, it would not be complete without talking about EDGE (An Extreme Degree of a God Encounter). When we first started KH, we would do quarterly youth ministry gatherings that engaged thousands of youth. We asked God to give us our own identity that represented our Kingdom mandate. After seeking God, He gave us EDGE. EDGE initially started out as just an evangelizing tool but quickly turned into a movement. A very bright and anointed young lady ran EDGE by the name of Kelly.

Kelly was the least likely candidate to be part of the KH family. She graduated from Columbia University with her master's degree and did not have youth ministry on her agenda. Kelly started off as my Special Projects Director, but moved very quickly to become my EDGE Director.

When we first started EDGE, we averaged over 500 youth. Currently EDGE impacts thousands of youth and teaches them how to go after the presence of God. We have seen great deliverances take place at EDGE, and many lives, in New York City and beyond, have been permanently changed by the power of God.

Looking back, I am so thankful that God graced me to be a part of such a great team of energetic and enthusiastic young leaders. I am confident that they are all going to be world changers through the gifts and talents that God has invested in them. Let's go Kingdom!

Kingdom Living Nuggets

- The people of Israel were trapped in the wilderness, not due to lack of direction, but wrong thinking.
- Joshua and Caleb responded out of a renewed mind.
- Our programs were about bringing the Kingdom into an environment.
- The earth moans and groans for the believer to come out of hiding and bring solutions.
- As a leader, I believe in allowing people to work in their strengths while they work on their weaknesses
- Once you become a believer, you must then renew your mind with God's Word.
- When God spoke to Moses about building the tabernacle he gave him a blueprint

CHAPTER 14

Kingdom Dominion

Luke 9:1-2 (KJV) – *Then he called his twelve disciples together and gave them the power and authority over all devils and to cure **diseases. And he sent them to preach the Kingdom of God and to heal the sick.***

The instructions God gave His disciples were simple: to preach the Kingdom. If we as believers hold to the claim of being Christ's disciples, then we must receive these as our instructions as well. In St. Luke chapter 9:1-2, Christ not only gave the disciples authority, but also commanded them to preach—or publicly proclaim—the Kingdom. They were to do so with demonstrations of healings and the working of miracles, thus implementing His laws to bring all things back into order. When you preach the message of the Kingdom, you are preaching healing, faith, deliverance, salvation and everything the Bible has to offer. Every situation that can possibly reside in the earth is answered through the Kingdom message. Jesus preached the Kingdom more than any other message in the entire Bible! We are to follow His example as followers of Christ.

Through this message, we understand that Christ has empowered us to bring correction in the earth. The disciples were the first recipients of this message. However, we are still connected to the mandate.

It's Time to Manifest

> **Romans 8:19** (AMP) – *For the earnest expectation of creation waits for the manifestation of the sons of God. For the creation was made subject to vanity,(vanity means disappointment and misery) not willingly, but by reason of him who hath subjected the same in hope. Because creation itself also shall be delivered from the bondage of corruption," (or moral decay, or ruins) "into the glorious liberty of the children of God.*

When you get saved, you are reinstated to the original intent of why God created you. That's where God gives you dominion—to govern, to rule, to control, to manage, to lead, to affect, and to impact. ***Those are the seven elements to having dominion.***

God not only gave you dominion over your household, but over the earth. Your Kingdom authority goes beyond your house, and beyond your state of habitation. Jesus showed us this when He offered to go and heal the centurion's servant. The centurion responded, "You don't have to go to where he is. You have so much power. You can speak the word only. You can just send the word—tell the body what to do, even though you're not in front of it."

> **Matt 8:5-10** (KJV) - *And when Jesus was entered into Capernaum, there came unto him a centurion, beseeching him, And saying, Lord, my servant lieth at home sick of the palsy, grievously tormented. And*

Jesus saith unto him, I will come and heal him. The centurion answered and said, Lord, I am not worthy that thou shouldest come under my roof: but speak the word only, and my servant shall be healed. For I am a man under authority, having soldiers under me: and I say to this man, Go, and he goeth; and to another, Come, and he cometh; and to my servant, Do this, and he doeth it. When Jesus heard it, he marvelled, and said to them that followed, Verily I say unto you, I have not found so great faith, no, not in Israel.

Everything Is Under My Control

Hebrews 2:5 (AMP) – *For it was not to angels that God subjected the habitable world of the future, of which we are speaking. It has been solemnly and earnestly said in a certain place, 'What is man that you are mindful of him, or the son of man that you graciously and helpfully care for and visit and look after him? For some little time you have ranked him lower than and inferior to the angels; you have crowned him with glory and honor and set him over the works of your hands. For you have put everything in subjection under his feet.*

Now in putting everything in subjection to man, He left nothing outside of man's control. So there is not an issue, a place, or a thing that you cannot control by the power of your words and through the image of God in you. Where you cannot be, your words have enough power to be. Your words put you on the scene. Our President, the Commander in Chief of the United States of America, does not go to war. But, from the

White House, he can give orders that go all the way across the world. That is power and authority.

Since that's true in the natural, imagine the power of that truth from a Kingdom perspective. The problem is that we are not exercising who God has called us to be. We want to come to church, feel good, and get an emotional high. Then we return week after week, no testimonies, no increase, no nothing. Noah preached the same thing for over a hundred years, because the people did not get the message.

There may be times when God wants you to hear and preach the same message over and over until you start getting the results as a citizen of the Kingdom and start actually having dominion.

The Word must be working in every aspect of your life. It must be moving. You have got to make sure that everything lines up with the Word of God, and if it does not line up with the Word of God, get rid of it, throw it out, excommunicate it, have nothing to do with it. It will only slow you down.

Earth's creation is desperate for the sons of God to speak and give it a commandment. As a matter of fact, it is called "liberty." When creation is not obeying the voice of a son or daughter of the Kingdom, it is in captivity. Why? It was created to find freedom at your command only. When you are in the Kingdom and walking according to the laws of the Kingdom, you command the earth to bring forth for the benefit of Kingdom advancement. That is what it was created to do. Jesus clearly demonstrated this by speaking to the wind, speaking to the trees, and speaking to the elements. He understood the power of being the Son of God.

All things that are in the earth come from the earth—whether it's a brick building or simply, a chair. All things come from the earth. God purposely trapped creation in the earth for you. This means that whatever you speak to must obey you. Why? Because it is part of God's creation, and God gave you Kingdom rule over the earth as stewards. When you trusted God for a house, it is not enough to just say, "I'm believing God," and think that God is going to just move and make it happen. As a believer, I admonish you to readjust your thinking a bit. If God has given you complete dominion and power when you speak to a piece or pieces of property, then that property must come into full alignment with the commandment. Why? It's made from the earth and is created to do what we say and tell it to do—through the power that is working in and through us in Jesus' name.

I will never forget a time I took a train into Manhattan and saw an apartment building in a very nice part of town. Of course, as an up and coming real estate mogul, I wanted to buy it! During that time in my life, God was introducing me to the principles of dominion. It seemed that God wanted me to "try out" the principles of dominion as it related to this piece of property. It was a property that had been vacant and needed some work to bring it back up to living conditions. Taking the somewhat limited knowledge I had of the Kingdom at that time, I went and laid hands on the property. I commanded the property not to sell to anyone other than me.

To make a long story short, time went by and I got involved in other real estate deals and totally forgot about the building until I decided to take another trip to the city and noticed the building again! The building was still vacant. I found out that, over the last couple of years, many buyers had interest and wanted to buy, but for some "reason," they were unable to close any deals. It was at that moment that I heard the Holy Spirit say, "Do you really want that building?" It took me a minute to think. I finally decided to release the building. A couple of months later, someone had totally rehabilitated and sold the building. Now some may say that that's just a coincidence, but I say that's dominion! When I speak to anything in the earth realm, it must be subject to my authority.

Another example would be money. Money is nothing but paper and cotton. Paper comes from trees (the earth), and trees are part of creation. Remember, when you speak to creation, it has to obey you. Stop spending your time complaining, and start speaking. We don't work for money; money works for us. Speak words of life that activate the Kingdom of God in the earth on your behalf.

How unfortunate is it that we have become accustomed to teaching people to depend on the preacher. If something doesn't happen like the preacher says it will, we get mad at the preacher. Yet it is our responsibility, as believers, to activate the power and dominion God has given us to bring our new homes, cars, and newly saved family members into manifested existence. That is our job. It is my job, though, as a preacher to teach you the Word of God and how to apply its principles so you can live a victorious life in the earth.

The purpose of understanding and exercising dominion is not to accumulate "stuff" or money. I'm trying to teach you how to use the Word of God to get your inheritance—joy, peace, health, wealth, and so on—and operate and function in the Kingdom. The power is between your lips, and when you speak, things must happen!

Numbers 14 tells us the people of Israel found giants in the land that God told them to go and possess. There will be times in your Christian walk that God will tell you to do something where you will face opposition. Just because there is opposition doesn't mean God did not give you the commandment to take it over.

When God tells you to do something, it is a repossessing of territory, whether it's natural territory, spiritual territory, or territory in the labor force. Wherever it is, it is a repossessing of territory. That's what Kingdom people do, we repossess what the enemy (after Christ) illegally holds on to and reproduce the laws and principles of the Kingdom of God to rule that sphere. We are preparing the earth for the reign of Christ.

Knowing this, expect the enemy to be intimidated when you understand the power of the authority that is in you. The enemy has some knowledge, a little inkling, that your success will be used for the Kingdom of God. Because of this, he will unleash unseemly opposition, even opposition we may not recognize as such. The enemy may try to use our lack of knowledge as a tool against us. He might try to attach our minds and give us an alternate mind set so that we do not walk in the things God has destined for us to walk in from the foundation of the world. The people of Israel had a slave mentality, and they kept saying, "Well, let's go back to the place with the Egyptians, because at least they'll give us our leeks and onions." The Israelites did not have to subject themselves to such negative thinking; all they had to do was walk into what God had already prepared for them.

> **Numbers14:6- 10** (version) – *And Joshua the son of Nun and Caleb the son of Jephunneh, which were of them that searched the land, rent their clothes: and they space unto all the company of the children of Israel, saying, 'The land, which we passed through to*

search it, is exceedingly good to eat. It's a good land. If the Lord delight in us, then he will bring us into the land, and give it to us; a land which flowed with milk and honey. Only rebel not ye against the Lord, neither fear ye the people of the land; for they are bread for us. Their defense is departed from them, and the Lord is with us: fear them not.' But all the congregation, bade stone them with stones. And the glory of the Lord appeared in the tabernacle of the congregation before all the children of Israel.

If God says that it—whatever the "it" may be in your life—is yours, then it is yours. If God said you could ask and it shall be given to you, or if you can speak to the mountains and command them to move, then you have the power to do this (Mark 11:22-23). This does not just work for the preachers. It works for whoever will believe. If you will believe, it's within your reach right now. Not later, but now. God wants to fill your barn until it overflows.

Kingdom Living Nuggets

- You demonstrate the Kingdom through healing, working of miracles and implementing Kingdom laws and principles wherever there is chaos.
- The earth is desperate to hear your voice.
- Speak words of life that activate the Kingdom of God in the earth on your behalf.
- When you get saved, you are reinstated to the original intent of why God created you.
- Where you cannot be, your words are.
- There will be times in your Christian walk when God will tell you to do something where opposition will try and stop you.
- The Word works for **whoever will believe**
- Kingdom people repossess what the enemy illegally holds
- Readjust your thinking

PART 5:
Finding Your Kingdom Purpose

CHAPTER 15

The Kingdom Action Blueprint

The dictionary defines *"blueprint"* as a detailed outline or plan of action. This chapter is designed to serve two purposes.

First, this document will help you to discover your area(s) of cultural influence. This can be discovered through many methods designed to reveal your gifts and talents. These gifts and talents are indicators of the location of your territory. Many times, due to the fear of failure, we are paralyzed. We are scared that if we move forward, we'll fall flat on our faces. My grandfather use to always say, "Whom the Lord calls, he qualifies" Stop focusing so much on your weaknesses and operate in your strengths. Everyone God told in the Bible to do a particular assignment had a weakness. When God spoke to Moses about setting the people of Israel free, Moses immediately started complaining about his weakness of speech. God is well aware of what you don't have. He calls you, however, for what you do have. Work on those weaknesses but go in the power of the strength you have.

Second, once you discover your gifts and talents, you need a plan of action in order to effectively influence those around you. No matter what industry you are in, you will be able to use some of these strategies to build influence. Please do not take this chapter lightly. This chapter has extreme value. Let's get started.

A. Discovering Your Sphere

The spheres are as follows:

Religion
- ☐ Church
- ☐ Missions
- ☐ 5-fold Ministries
- ☐ Bible School
- ☐ Discipleship

Family
- ☐ Marriage
- ☐ Parenting
- ☐ Motherhood/Fatherhood Roles
- ☐ Traditional Family Values

Government
- ☐ Local
- ☐ State
- ☐ National
- ☐ Military
- ☐ Law and Policy
- ☐ Lobbyists
- ☐ Ambassadors
- ☐ Social Services

Business
- ☐ Finance
- ☐ Manufacturing
- ☐ Retail
- ☐ Construction

- ☐ Sales
- ☐ Agriculture
- ☐ Health Care
- ☐ Transportation
- ☐ Food Industry
- ☐ Entrepreneurs

Media
- ☐ News Outlet
- ☐ Radio
- ☐ Journalism
- ☐ Marketing
- ☐ Public Speaking
- ☐ Technology

Art/Entertainment
- ☐ Theater/Fine Arts
- ☐ Dance
- ☐ Television
- ☐ Music
- ☐ Artisans
- ☐ Films
- ☐ Sports

Education
- ☐ Teachers/Professors
- ☐ Administration
- ☐ Curriculum
- ☐ Science
- ☐ Medicine
- ☐ Research
- ☐ Schools

These basic questions will help you get an idea where your sphere of influence is.

Complete the exercises below in your favorite journal.

Exercise 1

1. What are some of your favorite things to do?

2. What would you do, even if you did not get paid to do it?

3. What problems in society concern, anger, or trouble you every time you see or hear about it?

4. What are you passionate about?

5. Name several topics that fascinate you.

6. What industries are you most attracted to?

7. What topics do you love to read, write, and learn about?

Exercise 2

Part One: Make a list of all your various abilities and talents. No matter how big or small, name everything and anything that interests you. You'll be surprised at some of the things that will appear on your list.

Part Two: Write out all the things that God has been speaking or showing you in prayer—visions and dreams—concerning you. Even include prophetic words that have been spoken over your life by different men and women of God.

Part Three: Lastly, make a list of people, no matter their occupation, that you admire and have greatly influenced you. Be sure to explain, in detail, how each individual has influenced you.

When you complete this exercise, you will begin to see that your responses resonate with certain areas of cultural influence—whether it be in education, politics, theology, business, finance, accounting, art, fashion, counseling, family, and so on.

Note: You can find a spiritual gifts analysis at www.churchgrowth.org.

B. Creating a Blueprint of Influence

Once you know what territory God has called you to, it is important to gain influence in that arena. This section of the action plan is mainly for those, although it can benefit anyone, who may not have a pulpit ministry and do not know how to begin the process of operating in their area of Kingdom influence. Of course, as believers, prayer precedes all things! We can never abandon our prayer life and God's divine direction when making such determinations. In addition to acknowledging God, we must each equip ourselves with an adequate amount of knowledge. Gaining and providing knowledge in your field is extremely important. You are reading this book because I had to take the time to write it and get the message of the Kingdom out. No matter how great this message is, this book could not write itself.

Here are some key ideas and suggestions that will help you gain credibility and influence in your chosen fields as well as begin to build a blueprint for your Kingdom impact.

Note: Your sphere of influence does not have to be in the non-profit sector. Influence can be in any of the seven mountains mentioned in the previous chapters.

- Get educated in your spheres. This may involve going back to school and getting a degree or training certificate. Revelation correlates with one's level of knowledge. Functioning at the top of your area of influence takes great skill and preparation.
- Identify the problems that exist in your sphere and develop solutions.
- Adopt mentors and spiritual guidance from someone who has experience in your field. The Bible says to mark the "perfect man" (Psalms 37:37). It is very important to find someone who can help you avoid years of pain and mistakes. Mentors can help you accomplish this.
- Become part of an organization in your area of societal influence. For example, if you are an entrepreneur, join local business organizations.
- Build your influence and credibility by becoming an authority figure in your sphere. This can be done through a variety of channels, such as:
    - Authoring books
    - Becoming a columnist
    - Becoming a radio personality
    - Coaching
    - Consulting
    - Creating audio and video series
    - Developing websites that sell your products
    - Hosting seminars
    - Speaking engagements

These are just some of the ways to start building your blueprint for Kingdom advancement, prayerfully meditate on your strategy. I'm not sure who said it but I want to leave you with this quote I heard years ago:

"Passion tells you, what you should be doing, who you should be around, what you should be reading and how you should be acting."

This is your time to rule the earth for the Kingdom of God and impact the earth with the influence of heaven.

Key Kingdom Scriptural Reference

Luke 17:21- Neither shall they say, Lo here! or, lo there! For, behold, the kingdom of God is within you

Deuteronomy 8:7-9 (AMP) – For the Lord your God is bringing you into a good land, a land of brooks of water, of fountains and springs, flowing forth in valleys and hills; A land of wheat and barley, and vines and fig trees and pomegranates, a land of olive trees and honey; A land in which you shall eat food without shortage and lack nothing in it; a land whose stones are iron and out of whose hills you can dig copper.

Deuteronomy 28:10-13 (AMP) – And all people of the earth shall see that you are called by the name [and in the presence of] the Lord, and they shall be afraid of you. And the Lord shall make you have a surplus of prosperity, through the fruit of your body, of your livestock, and of your ground, in the land which the Lord swore to your fathers to give you. The Lord shall open to you His good treasury, the heavens, to give the rain of your land in its season and to bless all the work of your hands; and you shall lend to many nations, but you shall not borrow. And the Lord shall make you the head, and not the tail; and you shall be above only, and you shall not be beneath, if you heed the commandments of the Lord your God which I command you this day and are watchful to do them.

Daniel 6:7 (KJV) – All the presidents of the kingdom, the governors, and the princes, the counselors, and the captains, have consulted together to establish a royal statute, and to make a firm decree, that whosoever shall ask a petition of any God or man for thirty days, save of thee, O king, he shall be cast into the den of lions.

Luke 19:17-19 (AMP) – And he said to him, Well done, excellent bond servant! Because you have been faithful and trustworthy in a very little [thing], you shall have authority over ten cities. The second one also came and said, Lord, your mina has made five more minas. And he said also to him, and you will take charge over five cities.

Ephesians 3:10 (KJV) - To the intent that now unto the principalities and powers in heavenly places might be known by the church the manifold wisdom of God.

Genesis 41:38-41; 55-57 (KJV) - And Pharaoh said unto his servants, Can we find such a one as this is, a man in whom the Spirit of God is? And Pharaoh said unto Joseph, Forasmuch as God hath shewed thee all this, there is none so discreet and wise as thou art: Thou shalt be over my house, and according unto thy word shall all my people be ruled: only in the throne will I be greater than thou. And Pharaoh said unto Joseph, See, I have set thee over all the land of Egypt.

Isaiah 2:2 (AMP) – It shall come to pass in the latter days that the mountain of the Lord's house shall be [firmly] established as the highest of the mountains and shall be exalted above the hills, and all nations shall flow to it.

Proverbs 29:2 (KJV) – When the righteous are in authority, the people rejoice: but when the wicked beareth rule, the people mourn

Daniel 1:19-20 (KJV) – And the king communed with them; and among them all was found none like Daniel, Hananiah, Mishael, and Azariah: therefore stood they before the king. And in all matters of wisdom and understanding, that the king enquired of them, he found them ten times better than all the magicians and astrologers that were in all his realm

Deuteronomy 28:1-4, 8 – And it shall come to pass, if thou shalt hearken diligently unto the voice of the LORD thy God to observe and to do all His commandments which I command thee this day, that the LORD thy God will set thee on high above all nations of the earth; and all these blessings shall come on thee and overtake thee, if thou shalt hearken unto the voice of the LORD thy God: Blessed shalt thou be in the city, and blessed shalt thou be in the field. Blessed shall be the fruit of thy body, and the fruit of thy ground, and the fruit of thy herds, the increase of thy cattle, and the flocks of thy sheep...The LORD shall command the blessing upon thee in thy storehouses and in all that thou settest thine hand unto; and He shall bless thee in the land which the LORD thy God giveth thee.

Romans 8:19-21 – For the earnest expectation of the creature *(creatures in the original Greek means creation)* waits for the manifestation of the sons of God. For creation was made subject to vanity *(or misery, vanity means misery)* not willingly, but by reason of him who has subjected.

John 3:16a – For God so loved the world that he gave his only begotten Son...

Hebrews 2:7-8 (Amplified) - For some little time you have ranked him lower than and inferior to the angels; You have crowned him with glory and honor and set him over the works of Your hands, For You have put everything in subjection under his feet. Now in putting everything in subjection to man, He left nothing outside [of man's] control. But at present we do not yet see all things subjected to him [man].

Romans 8: 17-19 – For the manifestation of the sons of God, For the creature was made subject to vanity, not willingly, but by reason of him who has subjected the same in hope, because the creature itself also shall be delivered from the bondage of corruption into the glorious liberty of the children of God. For we know that the whole creation groaneth and travaileth in pain together until now."

Romans 5:17-19 (AMP) – For if because of one man's trespass *(lapse, offense)* death reigned through that one, much more surely will those who receive *[God's]* overflowing grace *(unmerited favor)* and the free gift of righteousness *[putting them into right standing with Himself]* reign as kings in life through the one Man Jesus Christ *(the Messiah, the Anointed One)*.

Daniel 2:44 – And in the days of these kings, the final ten kings, shall the God of Heaven set up a Kingdom, which shall never be destroyed, nor shall its sovereignty be left to another people, but it shall break and crush and consume all these kingdoms, and it shall stand forever.

2 Chronicles 20:25-28 – When Jehoshaphat and his people came to take the spoil, they found among them much cattle, goods, garments, precious things, which they took for themselves. And then they could carry away so much, that it took three days to gather all the spoil. They came to Jerusalem with harps, lyres and trumpets, to the house of God. And the fear of God came upon all the kingdom of those countries when they heard that the Lord had fought against the enemy of Israel.

Matthew 6:33 (AMP) – But seek (aim at and strive after) first of all His kingdom and His righteousness (His way of doing and being right), and then all these things taken together will be given you besides

Genesis 1:26-28 (AMP) – God said, Let Us [Father, Son, and Holy Spirit] make mankind in Our image, after Our likeness, and let them have complete authority over the fish of the sea, the birds of the air, the [tame] beasts, and over all of the earth, and over everything that creeps upon the earth. So God created man in His own image, in the image and likeness of God He created him; male and female He created them. And God blessed them and said to them, be fruitful, multiply, and fill the earth, and subdue it [using all its vast resources in the service of God and man]; and have dominion over the fish of the sea, the birds of the air, and over every living creature that moves upon the earth.

Ephesians 2:19 (AMP) – Therefore you are no longer outsiders (exiles, migrants, and aliens, excluded from the rights of citizens), but you now share **citizenship** with the saints (God's own people, consecrated and set apart for Himself); and you belong to God's [own] household. This was the beginning of a journey in which I am still on today. This journey has caused me to write this book and preach the gospel of Jesus Christ not just salvation.

Colossians 1:13 (AMP) – [The Father] has delivered and drawn us to Himself out of the control and the dominion of darkness and has transferred us into the kingdom of the Son of His love,

Psalm 115:16 (KJV) – The heaven, even the heavens, are the LORD's: but the earth hath he given to the children of men.

Matthew 12:28-29, (AMP) – *But if it is by the Spirit of God that I drive out the demons, then the Kingdom of God has come upon you before you expected it*

Exodus 23: 20-23, 25 (KJV) – Behold, I sent an angel before you to keep you and to guard you along the way, and to bring you to the place which I have prepared unto you. Give heed to him, listen to him, obey him. But if you do not listen to him and obey his voice that I speak, I will put an enemy to your enemies. You shall serve the Lord your God, he shall bless your bread and your water, and I will take sickness from the midst of you. None shall lose her young by miscarriage or the barren in your land. I will fulfill the number of your days.

Nehemiah 9:19-22 (KJV) – Yet though in thy manifold mercies forsookest them not in the wilderness. The pillar of cloud departed not from them by day, to lead them in the way, neither the pillar of fire by night, to shew them light and the way wherein they should go. Yeah, 40 years didst thou sustain them in the wilderness so that they lacked nothing. Their clothes waxed not old, and their feet swelled not. Moreover, thou gavest us them kingdoms and nations.

Matthew 13: 37-43 (KJV) - He answered and said unto them, He that soweth the good seed is the Son of man; The field is the world; the good seed are the children of the kingdom; but the tares are the children of the wicked one; The enemy that sowed them is the devil; the harvest is the end of the world; and the reapers are the angels. As therefore the tares are gathered and burned in the fire; so shall it be in the end of this world. The Son of man shall send forth his angels, and they shall gather out of his kingdom all things that offend, and them which do iniquity; And shall cast them into a furnace of fire: there shall be wailing and gnashing of teeth. Then shall the righteous shine forth as the sun in the kingdom of their Father. Who hath ears to hear, let him hear.

Luke 9:1-2 (KJV) – Then he called his twelve disciples together and gave them the power and authority over all devils and to cure diseases. And he sent them to preach the Kingdom of God and to heal the sick.

If you would like to contact
ANDRE R JONES
for speaking engagements:

Write: ANDRE R JONES
                     P.O Box 10649,
                     Westbury, New York 11590

Call: (888) 618-7690

Visit Our Website: www.AndreRJones.com

Social Media: Friend us on Facebook,
                     Follow us on Twitter

Personal Notes

Personal Notes

Personal Notes

www.ingramcontent.com/pod-product-compliance
Lightning Source LLC
Chambersburg PA
CBHW072042290426
44110CB00014B/1557